WHERE
NO FEAR WAS

WHERE NO FEAR WAS

A BOOK ABOUT FEAR

ARTHUR CHRISTOPHER BENSON

GYAN

Published by

Gyan Publishing House
5, Ansari Road
Daryaganj, New Delhi-110002
Phone: 011-47034999, 9811692060
E-mail: books@gyanbooks.com

Distribution Network
gyanbooks.com
India, USA, Canada, UK, Australia, France

ISBN: 978-81-212-9108-8 (PB)
First Published, 1907

2nd Impression 2023

Printed at: Gyan Press, Delhi.

WHERE NO FEAR WAS
AUTHOR: ARTHUR CHRISTOPHER BENSON

WHERE NO FEAR WAS

WHERE NO FEAR WAS

A BOOK ABOUT FEAR

BY

ARTHUR CHRISTOPHER BENSON

LONDON
SMITH, ELDER & CO., 15 WATERLOO PLACE
1914

CONTENTS

		PAGE
I.	The Shadow	1
II.	Shapes of Fear	8
III.	The Darkest Doubt	15
IV.	Vulnerability	20
V.	The Use of Fear	30
VI.	Fears of Childhood	39
VII.	Fears of Boyhood	54
VIII.	Fears of Youth	68
IX.	Fears of Middle Age	77
X.	Fears of Age	88
XI.	Dr. Johnson	106
XII.	Tennyson, Ruskin, Carlyle	119
XIII.	Charlotte Brontë	140
XIV.	John Sterling	155
XV.	Instinctive Fear	162
XVI.	Fear of Life	178
XVII.	Simplicity	195
XVIII.	Affection	204
XIX.	Sin	213
XX.	Serenity	225

"Thus they went on till they came to about the middle of the Valley, and then Christiana *said, 'Methinks I see something yonder on the road before us, a thing of such a shape such as I have not seen.' Then said* Joseph, *'Mother, what is it?' 'An ugly thing, Child, an ugly thing,' said she. 'But, Mother, what is it like?' said he. ''Tis like I cannot tell what,' said she. And now it was but a little way off. Then said she, 'It is nigh.'"*

—*"Pilgrim's Progress," Part II.*

WHERE NO FEAR WAS

I

THE SHADOW

THERE surely may come a time for each of us, if we have lived with any animation or interest, if we have had any constant or even fitful desire to penetrate and grasp the significance of the strange adventure of life, a time, I say, when we may look back a little, not sentimentally or with any hope of making out an impressive case for ourselves, and interrogate the memory as to what have been the most real, vivid, and intense things that have befallen us by the way. We may try to separate the momentous from the trivial, and the important from the unimportant; to discern where and how and when we might have acted differently; to see and to say what has really mattered, what has made a deep mark on our spirit; what has hampered or wounded or maimed us. Because one of the strangest things about life seems to be our incapacity to decide beforehand, or even at the time, where the real and fruitful joys, and where the dark dangers and distresses lie. The things that at certain times filled all one's mind, kindled hope and aim, seemed so infinitely desirable, so necessary to happiness, have faded, many of them, into the lightest and most worthless of husks and phantoms, like the withered flowers that we find sometimes shut in the pages of our old books, and cannot even remember of what glowing and emotional moment they were the record!

How impossible it is ever to learn anything by being told it! How necessary it is to pay the full price for any knowledge worth having! The anxious father, the tearful mother, may warn the little boy before he goes to school of the dangers that await him. He does not understand, he does not attend, he is looking at the pattern of the carpet, and wondering for the hundredth time whether the oddly-shaped blue thing which appears and reappears at intervals is a bird or a flower—yes, it is certainly meant for a bird perched on a bough! He wishes the talk were over, he looks at the little scar on his father's hand, and remembers that he has been told that he cut it in a cucumber-frame when he was a boy. And then, long afterwards perhaps, when he has made a mistake and is suffering for it, he sees that it was *that* of which they spoke, and wonders that they could not have explained it better.

And this is so all along! We cannot recognise the dark tower, to which in the story Childe Roland came, by any description. We must go there ourselves; and not till we feel the teeth of the trap biting into us, do we see that it was exactly in such a place that we had been warned that it would be laid.

There is an episode in that strange and beautiful book *Phantastes*, by George Macdonald, which comes often to my mind. The boy is wandering in the enchanted forest, and he is told to avoid the house where the Daughter of the Ogre lives. His morose young guide shows him where the paths divide, and he takes the one indicated to him with a sense of misgiving.

A little while before he had been deceived by

the Alder-maiden, and had given her his love in error. This has taken some of the old joy out of his heart, but he has made his escape from her, and thinks he has learned his lesson.

But he comes at last to the long low house in the clearing; he finds within it an ancient woman reading out of an old volume; he enters, he examines the room in which she sits, and yielding to curiosity, he opens the door of the great cupboard in the corner, in spite of a muttered warning. He thinks, on first opening it, that it is just a dark cupboard; but he sees with a shock of surprise that he is looking into a long dark passage, which leads out, far away from where he stands, into the starlit night. Then a figure, which seems to have been running from a long distance, turns the corner, and comes speeding down towards him. He has not time to close the door, but stands aside to let it pass; it passes, and slips behind him; and soon he sees that it is a shadow of himself, which has fallen on the floor at his feet. He asks what has happened, and then the old woman says that he has found his shadow, a thing which happens to many people; and then for the first time she raises her head and looks at him, and he sees that her mouth is full of long white teeth; he knows where he is at last, and stumbles out, with the dark shadow at his heels, which is to haunt him so miserably for many a sad day.

That is a very fine and true similitude of what befalls many men and women. They go astray, they give up some precious thing——their innocence perhaps—to a deluding temptation. They are delivered for a time; and then a little while after they find their shadow, which no tears or anguish of regret can take away, till the healing of life and work and purpose annuls it. Neither is it always annulled, even in length of days.

But it is a paltry and inglorious mistake to let the shadow have its disheartening will of us. It is only a shadow, after all! And if we capitulate after our first disastrous encounter, it does not mean that we shall be for ever vanquished, though it means perhaps a long and dreary waste of shame-stained days. That is what we must try to avoid—any *waste* of time and strength. For if anything is certain, it is that we have all to fight until we conquer, and the sooner we take up the dropped sword again the better.

And we have also to learn that no one can help us except ourselves. Other people can sympathise and console, try to soothe our injured vanity, try to persuade us that the dangers and disasters ahead are not so dreadful as they appear to be, and that the mistakes we have made are not irreparable. But no one can remove danger or regret from us, or relieve us of the necessity of facing our own troubles ; the most that they can do, indeed, is to encourage us to try again.

But we cannot hope to change the conditions of life ; and one of its conditions is, as I have said, that we cannot foresee dangers. No matter how vividly they are described to us, no matter how eagerly those who love us try to warn us of peril, we cannot escape. For that is the essence of life—experience ; and though we cannot rejoice when we are in the grip of it, and when we cannot see what the end will be, we can at least say to ourselves again and again, "this is at all events reality—this is business!" for it is the moments of endurance and energy and action which after all justify us in living, and not the pleasant spaces where we saunter among flowers and sunlit woods. Those are conceded to us, to tempt us to live, to make us desire to remain in the world; and we need not be afraid to take them, to use them, to enjoy them; because all things alike help to make us what we are.

II

SHAPES OF FEAR

Now as I look back a little, I see that some of my worst experiences have not hurt or injured me at all. I do not claim more than my share of troubles, but "I have had trouble enough for one," as Browning says,—bereavements, disappointments, the illness of those I have loved, illness of my own, quarrels, misunderstandings, enmities, angers, disapprovals, losses; I have made bad mistakes, I have failed in my duty, I have done many things that I regret, I have been unreasonable, unkind, selfish. Many of these things have hurt and wounded me, have brought me into sorrow, and even into despair. But I do not feel that any of them have really injured me, and some of them have already benefited me. I have learned to be a little more patient and diligent, and I have discovered that there are certain things that I must at all costs avoid.

But there is one thing which seems to me to have always and invariably hampered and maimed me, whenever I have yielded to it, and I have often yielded to it; and that is Fear. It can be called by many names, and all of them ugly names—anxiety, timidity, moral cowardice. I can never trace the smallest good in having given way to it. It has been from my earliest days the Shadow; and I think it is the shadow in the lives of many men and women. I want in this book to track it, if I can, to its lair, to see what it is, where its awful power lies, and what, if anything, one can do to resist it. It seems the most unreal thing in the world, when one is on the other side of it; and yet face to face with it, it has a strength, a poignancy, a paralysing power, which makes it seem like a personal and specific ill-will, issuing in a sort of dreadful enchantment or spell, which renders it impossible to withstand. Yet, strange to say, it has not exercised its power in the few occasions in my life when it would seem to have been really justified. Let me quote an instance or two which will illustrate what I mean.

I was confronted once with the necessity of a small surgical operation, quite unexpectedly. If I had known beforehand that it was to be done, I should have depicted every incident with horror and misery. But the moment arrived, and I found myself marching to my bedroom with a surgeon and a nurse, with a sense almost of amusement at the adventure.

I was called upon once in Switzerland to assist with two guides in the rescue of an unfortunate woman who had fallen from a precipice, and had to be brought down, dead or alive. We hurried up through the pine-forest with a chair, and found the poor creature alive indeed, but with horrible injuries—an eye knocked out, an arm and a thigh broken, her ulster torn to ribbons, and with more blood about the place in pools than I should have thought a human body could contain. She was conscious; she had to be lifted into the chair, and we had to discover where she belonged; she fainted away in the middle of it, and I had to go on and break the news to her relations. If I had been told beforehand what would have had to be done, I do not think I could have faced it; but it was there to do, and I found myself entirely capable of taking part, and even of wondering all the time that it was possible to act.

Again, I was once engulfed in a crevasse, hanging from the ice-ledge with a portentous gulf below, and a glacier-stream roaring in the darkness. I could get no hold for foot or hand, my companions could not reach me or extract me; and as I sank into unconsciousness, hearing my own expiring breath, I knew that I was doomed; but I can only say, quite honestly and humbly, that I had no fear at all, and only dimly wondered what arrangements would be made at Eton, where I was then a master, to accommodate the boys of my house and my pupils. It was not done by an effort, nor did I brace myself to the situation: fear simply did not come near to me.

Once again I found myself confronted, not so long ago, with an incredibly painful and distressing interview. That indeed did oppress me with almost intolerable dread beforehand. I was to go to a certain house in London, and there was just a chance that the interview might not take place after all. As I drove there, I suddenly found myself wondering whether the interview could *really* be going to take place — how often had I rehearsed it beforehand with anguish—and then as suddenly became aware that I should in some strange way be disappointed if it did not take place. I wanted on the whole to go through with it, and to see what it would be like. A deep-seated curiosity came to my aid. It did take place, and it was very bad—worse than I could have imagined; but it was not terrible!

These are just four instances which come into my mind. I should be glad to feel that the courage which undoubtedly came had been the creation of my will; but it was not so. In three cases, the events came unexpectedly; but in the fourth case I had long anticipated the moment with extreme dread. Yet in that last case the fear suddenly slipped away, without the smallest effort on my part; and in all four cases some strange gusto of experience, some sense of heightened life and adventure, rose in the mind like a fountain—so that even in the crevasse I said to myself, not excitedly but serenely, "So this is what it feels like to await death!"

It was this particular experience which gave me an inkling into that which in so many tragic histories seems incredible — that men often do pass to death, by scaffold and by stake, at the last moment, in serenity and even in joy. I do not doubt for a moment that it is the immortal principle in man, the sense of deathlessness, which comes to his aid. It is the instinct which, in spite of all knowledge and experience, says suddenly, in a moment like that, "Well, what then?" That instinct is a far truer thing than any expectation or imagination. It sees things, in supreme moments, in a true proportion. It asserts that when the rope jerks, or the flames leap up, or the benumbing blow falls, there is something there which cannot possibly be injured, and which indeed is rather freed from the body of our humiliation. It is but an incident, after all, in a much longer and more momentous voyage. It means only the closing of one chapter of experience and the beginning of another. The base element in it is the fear which dreads the opening of the door, and the quitting of what is familiar. And I feel assured of this, that the one universal and inevitable experience, known to us as death, must in reality be a very simple and even a natural affair, and that when we can look back upon it, it will seem to us amazing that we can ever have regarded it as so momentous and appalling a thing.

III

THE DARKEST DOUBT

Now we can make no real advance in the things of the spirit until we have seen what lies on the other side of fear; fear cannot help us to grow, at best it can only teach us to be prudent; it does not of itself destroy the desire to offend—only shame can do that; if our wish to be different comes merely from our being afraid to transgress, then, if the fear of punishment were to be removed, we should go back with a light heart to our old sins. We may obey irresponsible power, because we know that it can hurt us if we disobey; but unless we can perceive the reason why this and that is forbidden, we cannot concur with law. We learn as children that flame has power to hurt us, but we only dread the fire because it can injure us, not because we admire the reason which it has for burning.

So long as we do not sin simply because we know the laws of life which punish sin, we have not learned any hatred of sin ; it is only because we hate the punishment more than we love the sin, that we abstain.

Socrates once said, in one of his wise paradoxes, that it was better to sin knowingly than ignorantly. That is a hard saying, but it means that at least if we sin knowingly, there is some purpose, some courage in the soul. We take a risk with our eyes open, and our purpose may perhaps be changed ; whereas if we sin ignorantly, we do so out of a mere base instinct, and there is no purpose that may be educated. Anyone who has ever had the task of teaching boys or young men to write will know how much easier it is to teach those who write volubly and exuberantly, and desire to express themselves, even if they do it with many faults and lapses of taste ; taste and method may be corrected, if only the instinct of expression is there. But the young man who has no impulse to write, who says that he could think of nothing to say, it is impossible to teach him much, because one cannot communicate the desire for expression.

And the same holds good of life. Those who have strong vital impulses can learn restraint and choice; but the people who have no particular impulses and preferences, who just live out of mere impetus and habit, who plod along, doing in a dispirited way just what they find to do, and lapsing into indolence and indifference the moment that prescribed work ceases, those are the spirits that afford the real problem, because they despise activity, and think energy a mere exhibition of fussy diffuseness.

But the generous, eager, wilful nature, who has always some aim in sight, who makes mistakes perhaps, gives offence, collides high-heartedly with others, makes both friends and enemies, loves and hates, is anxious, jealous, self-absorbed, resentful, intolerant—there is always hope for such an one, for he is quick to despair, capable of shame, swift to repent, and even when he is worsted and wounded, rises to fight again. Such a nature, through pain and love, can learn to chasten his base desires, and to choose the nobler and worthier way.

But what does really differentiate men and women is not their power of fearing and suffering, but their power of caring and admiring. The only real and vital force in the world is the force which attracts, the beauty which is so desirable that one must imitate it if one can, the wisdom which is so calm and serene that one must possess it if one may.

And thus all depends upon our discerning in the world a loving intention of some kind, which holds us in view, and draws us to itself. If we merely think of God and nature as an inflexible system of laws, and that our only chance of happiness is to slip in and out of them, as a man might pick his way among red-hot ploughshares, thankful if he can escape burning, then we can make no sort of advance, because we can have neither faith nor trust. The thing from which one merely flees can have no real power over our spirit; but if we know God as a fatherly Heart behind nature, who is leading us on our way, then indeed we can walk joyfully in happiness, and undismayed in trouble; because troubles then become only the wearisome incidents of the upward ascent, the fatigue, the failing breath, the strained muscles, the discomfort which is actually taking us higher, and cannot by any means be avoided.

But fear is the opposite of all this; it is the dread of the unknown, the ghastly doubt as to whether there is any goal before us or not; when we fear, we are like the butterfly that flutters anxiously away from the boy who pursues it, who means out of mere wantonness to strike it down tattered and bruised among the grass-stems.

IV

VULNERABILITY

THERE have been many attempts in the history of mankind to escape from the dominion of fear; the essence of fear, that which prompts it, is the consciousness of our vulnerability. What we all dread is the disease or the accident that may disable us, the loss of money or credit, the death of those whom we love and whose love makes the sunshine of our life, the anger and hostility and displeasure and scorn and ill-usage of those about us. These are the definite things which the anxious mind forecasts, and upon which it mournfully dwells.

The object then in the minds of the philosophers or teachers who would fain relieve the unhappiness of the world, has been always to suggest ways in which this vulnerability may be lessened; and thus their object has been to disengage as far as possible the hopes and affections of men from things which must always be fleeting. That is the principle which lies behind all asceticism, that, if one can be indifferent to wealth and comfort and popularity, one has a better chance of serenity. The essence of that teaching is not that pleasant things are not desirable, but that one is more miserable if one loses them than if one never cares for them at all. The ascetic trains himself to be indifferent about food and drink and the apparatus of life; he aims at celibacy partly because love itself is an overmastering passion, and partly because he cannot bear to engage himself with human affections, the loss of which may give him pain. There is, of course, a deeper strain in asceticism than this, which is a suspicious mistrust of all physical joys and a sense of their baseness; but that is in itself an artistic preference of mental and spiritual joys, and a defiance to everything which may impair or invade them.

The Stoic imperturbability is an attempt to take a further step; not to fly from life, but to mingle with it, and yet to grow to be not dependent on it. The Stoic ideal was a high one, to cultivate a firmness of mind that was on the one hand not to be dismayed by pain or suffering, and on the other to use life so temperately and judiciously as not to form habits of indulgence which it would be painful to discontinue. The weakness of Stoicism was that it despised human relations; and the strength of primitive Christianity was that, while it recommended a Stoical simplicity of life, it taught men not to be afraid of love, but to use and lavish love freely, as being the one thing which would survive death and not be cut short by it. The Christian teaching came to this, that the world was meant to be a school of love, and that love was to be an outward-rippling ring of affection textending from the family outwards to the tribe, the nation, the world, and on to God Himself. It laid all its emphasis on the truth that love is the one immortal thing, that all the joys and triumphs of the world pass away with the decay of its material framework, but that love passes boldly on, with linked hands, into the darkness of the unknown.

The one loss that Christianity recognised was

the loss of love; the one punishment it dreaded was the withholding of love.

As Christianity soaked into the world, it became vitiated, and drew into itself many elements of human weakness. It became a social force, it learned to depend on property, it fulminated a code of criminality, and accepted human standards of prosperity and wealth. It lost its simplicity and became sophisticated. It is hard to say that men of the world should not, if they wish, claim to be Christians, but the whole essence of Christianity is obscured if it is forgotten that its vital attributes are its indifference to material conveniences, and its emphatic acceptance of sympathy as the one supreme virtue.

This is but another way of expressing that our troubles and our terrors alike are based on selfishness, and that if we are really concerned with the welfare of others we shall not be much concerned with our own.

The difficulty in adopting the Christian theory is that God does not apparently intend to cure the world by creating all men unselfish. People are born selfish, and the laws of nature and heredity seem to ordain that it shall be so. Indeed a certain selfishness seems to be inseparable from any desire to live. The force of asceticism and of Stoicism is that they both appeal to selfishness as a motive. They frankly say, "Happiness is your aim, personal happiness; but instead of grasping at pleasure whenever it offers, you will find it more prudent in the end not to care too much about such things." It is true that popular Christianity makes the same sort of appeal. It says, or seems to say, "If you grasp at happiness in this world, you may secure a great deal of it successfully; but it will be worse for you eventually."

The theory of life as taught and enforced, for instance, in such a work as Dante's great poem is based upon this crudity of thought. Dante, by his Hell and his Purgatory, expressed plainly that the chief motive of man to practise morality must be his fear of ultimate punishment. His was an attempt to draw away the curtain which hides this world from the next, and to horrify men into living purely and kindly. But the mind only revolts against the dastardly injustice of a God, who allows men to be born into the world so corrupt, with so many incentives to sin, and deliberately hides from them the ghastly sight of the eternal torments, which might have saved them from recklessness of life. No one who had trod the dark caverns of Hell or the flinty ridges of Purgatory, as Dante represented himself doing, who had seen the awful sights and heard the heart-broken words of the place, could have returned to the world as a light-hearted sinner! Whatever we may believe of God, we must not for an instant allow ourselves to believe that life can be so brief and finite, so small and hampered an opportunity, and that punishment could be so demoniacal and so infinite. A God who could design such a scheme must be essentially evil and malignant. We may menace wicked men with punishment for wanton misdeeds, but it must be with just punishment. What could we say of a human father who exposed a child to temptation without explaining the consequences, and then condemned him to lifelong penalties for failing to make the right choice? We must firmly believe that if offences are finite, punishment must be finite too; that it must be remedial and not mechanical. We must believe that if we deserve punishment, it will be because we can hope for restoration. Hell is a monstrous and insupportable fiction, and the idea of it is simply inconsistent with any belief in the goodness of God. It is easy to quote texts to support it, but we must not allow any text, any record in the world, however sacred, to shatter our belief in the Love and Justice of God. And I say as frankly and directly as I can that until we can get rid of this intolerable terror, we can make no advance at all.

The old, fierce Saints, who went into the darkness exulting in the thought of the eternal damnation of the wicked, had not spelt the first letter of the Christian creed, and I doubt not have discovered their mistake long ago! Yet there are pious people in the world who will neither think nor speak frankly of the subject, for fear of weakening the motives for human virtue. I will at least speak frankly, and though I believe with all my heart in a life beyond the grave, in which suffering enough may exist for the cure of those who by wilful sin have sunk into sloth and hopelessness and despair, and even into cruelty and brutality, I do not for an instant believe that the conduct of the vilest human being who ever set foot on the earth can deserve more than a term of punishment, or that such punishment will have anything that is vindictive about it.

It may be said that I am here only combating an old-fashioned idea, and that no one believes in the old theory of eternal punishment, or that if they believe that the possibility exists, they do not believe that any human being can incur it. But I feel little doubt that the belief does exist, and that it is more widespread than one cares to believe. To believe it is to yield to the darkest and basest temptation of fear, and keeps all who hold it back from the truth of God.

What then are we to believe about the punishment of our sins? I look back upon my own life, and I see numberless occasions—they rise up before me, a long perspective of failures—when I have acted cruelly, selfishly, self-indulgently, basely, knowing perfectly well that I was so behaving. What was wrong with me? Why did I so behave? Because I preferred the baser course, and thought at the time that it gave me pleasure.

Well then, what do I wish about all that? I wish it had not happened so, I wish I had been kinder, more just, more self-restrained, more strong. I am ashamed, because I condemn myself, and because I know that those whom I love and honour would condemn me, if they knew all. But I do not, therefore, lose all hope of myself, nor do I think that God will not show me how to be different. If it can only be done by suffering, I dread the suffering, but I am ready to suffer if I can become what I should wish to be. But I do not for a moment think that God will cast me off or turn His face away from me because I have sinned; and I can pray that He will lead me into light and strength.

And thus it is not my vulnerability that I dread; I rather welcome it as a sign that I may learn the truth so. And I will not look upon my desire for pleasant things as a proof that I am evil, but rather as a proof that God is showing me where happiness lies, and teaching me by my mistakes to discern and value it. He could make me perfect if He would, in a single instant. But the fact that He does not, is a sign that He has something better in store for me than a mere mechanical perfection.

V

THE USE OF FEAR

THE advantages of the fearful temperament, if it is not a mere unmanning and desolating dread, are not to be overlooked. Fear is the shadow of the imaginative, the resourceful, the inventive temperament, but it multiplies resource and invention a hundredfold. Everyone knows the superstition which is deeply rooted in humanity, that a time of exaltation and excitement and unusual success is held to be often the prelude to some disaster, just as the sense of excitement and buoyant health, when it is very consciously perceived, is thought to herald the approach of illness. "I felt so happy," people say, "that I was sure that some misfortune was going to befall me—it is not lucky to feel so secure as that!" This represented itself to the Greeks as part of the divine government of the world; they thought that the heedless and self-confident man was beguiled by success into what they called ὕβρις, the insolence of prosperity; and that then ἄτη, that is, disaster, followed. They believed that the over-prosperous man incurred the envy and jealousy of the gods. We see this in the old legend of Polycrates of Samos, whose schemes all succeeded, and whose ventures all turned out well. He consulted a soothsayer about his alarming prosperity, who advised him to inflict some deliberate loss or sacrifice upon himself; so Polycrates drew from his finger and flung into the sea a signet-ring which he possessed, with a jewel of great rarity and beauty in it. Soon afterwards a fish was caught by the royal fisherman, and was served up at the king's table —there, inside the body of the fish, was the ring; and when Polycrates saw that, he felt that the gods had restored him his gift, and that his destruction was determined upon; which came true, for he was caught by pirates at sea, and crucified upon a rocky headland.

No nation, and least of all the Greeks, would have arrived at this theory of life and fate, if they had not felt that it was supported by actual instances. It was of the nature of an inference from the facts of life; and the explanation undoubtedly is that men do get betrayed, by a constant experience of good fortune, into rashness and heedlessness, because they trust to their luck and depend upon their fortunate star.

But the man who is of an energetic and active type, if he is haunted by anxiety, if his imagination paints the possibilities of disaster, takes every means in his power to foresee contingencies, and to deal cautiously and thoroughly with the situation which causes him anxiety. If he is a man of keen sensibilities, the pressure of such care is so insupportable that he takes prompt and effective measures to remove it; and his fear thus becomes an element in his success, because it urges him to action, and at the same time teaches him the need of due precaution. As Horace wrote:

> "Sperat infestis, metuit secundis
> Alteram sortem."

"He hopes for a change of fortune when things are menacing, he fears a reverse when things are prosperous." And if we look at the facts of life, we see that it is not by any means the confident and optimistic people who succeed best in their designs. It is rather the man of eager and ambitious temperament, who dreads a repulse and anticipates it, and takes all possible measures beforehand to avoid it.

We see the same principle underlying the scientific doctrine of evolution. People often think loosely that the idea of evolution, in the case, let us say, of a bird like a heron, with his immobility, his long legs, his pointed beak, his muscular neck, is that such characteristics have been evolved through long ages by birds that have had to get their food in swamps and shallow lakes, and were thus gradually equipped for food-getting through long ages of practice. But of course no particular bird is thus modified by circumstances. A pigeon transferred to a fen would not develop the characteristics of the heron; it would simply die for lack of food. It is rather that certain minute variations take place, for unknown reasons, in every species; and the bird which happened to be hatched out in a fenland with a rather sharper beak or rather longer legs than his fellows, would have his power of obtaining food slightly increased, and would thus be more likely to perpetuate in his offspring that particular advantage of form. This principle working through endless centuries would tend slowly to develop the stock that was better equipped for life under such circumstances, and to eliminate those less suited to the locality; and thus the fittest would tend to survive. But it does not indicate any design on the part of the birds themselves, nor any deliberate attempt to develop those characteristics; it is rather that such characteristics, once started by natural variation, tend to emphasize themselves in the lapse of time.

No doubt fear has played an enormous part in the progress of the human race itself. The savage whose imagination was stronger than that of other savages, and who could forecast the possibilities of disaster, would wander through the forest with more precaution against wild beasts, and would make his dwelling more secure against assault; so that the more timid and imaginative type would tend to survive longest and to multiply their stock. Man in his physical characteristics is a very weak, frail, and helpless animal, exposed to all kinds of dangers; his infancy is protracted and singularly defenceless; his pace is slow, his strength is insignificant; it is his imagination that has put him at the top of creation, and has enabled him both to evade dangers and to use natural forces for his greater security. Though he is the youngest of all created forms, and by no means the best equipped for life, he has been able to go ahead in a way denied to all other animals; his inventiveness has been largely developed by his terrors; and the result has been that whereas all other animals still preserve, as a condition of life, their ceaseless attitude of suspicion and fear, man has been enabled by organisation to establish communities in which fear of disaster plays but little part. If one watches a bird feeding on a lawn, it is strange to observe its ceaseless vigilance. It takes a hurried mouthful, and then looks round in an agitated manner to see that it is in no danger of attack. Yet it is clear that the terror in which all wild animals seem to live, and without which self-preservation would be impossible, does not in the least militate against their physical welfare. A man who had to live his life under the same sort of risks that a bird in a garden has to endure from cats and other foes, would lose his senses from the awful pressure of terror; he would lie under the constant shadow of assassination.

But the singular thing in Nature is that she preserves characteristics long after they have ceased to be needed; and so, though a man in a civilised community has very little to dread, he is still haunted by an irrational sense of insecurity and precariousness. And thus many of our fears arise from old inheritance, and represent nothing rational or real at all, but only an old and savage need of vigilance and wariness.

One can see this exemplified in a curious way in level tracts of country. Everyone who has traversed places like the plain of Worcestershire must remember the irritating way in which the roads keep ascending little eminences, instead of going round at the foot. Now these old country roads no doubt represent very ancient tracks indeed, dating from times when much of the land was uncultivated. They get stereotyped, partly because they were tracks, and partly because for convenience the first enclosures and tillages were made along the roads for purposes of communication. But the perpetual tendency to ascend little eminences no doubt dates from a time when it was safer to go up, in order to look round and to see ahead, partly in order to be sure of one's direction, and partly to beware of the manifold dangers of the road.

And thus many of the fears by which one is haunted are these old survivals, these inherited anxieties. Who does not know the frame of mind when perhaps for a day, perhaps for days together, the mind is oppressed and uneasy, scenting danger in the air, forecasting calamity, recounting all the possible directions in which fate or malice may have power to wound and hurt us? It is a melancholy inheritance, but it cannot be combated by any reason. It is of no use then to imitate Robinson Crusoe, and to make a list of one's blessings on a piece of paper; that only increases our fear, because it is just the chance of forfeiting such blessings of which we are in dread! We must simply remind ourselves that we are surrounded by old phantoms, and that we derive our weakness from ages far back, in which risks were many and security was rare.

VI

FEARS OF CHILDHOOD

IF I look back over my own life, I can discern three distinct stages of fear and anxieties, and I expect it is the same with most people. The terrors of childhood are very mysterious things, and their horror consists in the child's inability to put the dread into words. I remember how one night, when we were living in the Master's Lodge at Wellington College, I had gone to bed, and waking soon afterwards heard a voice somewhere outside. I got out of bed, went to the door, and looked out. Close to my door was an archway which looked into the open gallery that ran round the big front hall, giving access to the bedrooms. At the opposite end of the hall, in the gallery, burnt a gaslight: to my horror I observed close to the gas what seemed to me a colossal shrouded statue, made of a black bronze, formless, silent, awful. I crept back to my bed, and there shivered in an ecstasy of fear, till at last I fell asleep. There was no statue there in the morning! I told my old nurse, after a day or two of dumb dread, what I had seen. She laughed, and told me that a certain Mrs. Holder, an elderly widow who was a dressmaker, had been to see her, about some piece of work. They had turned out the nursery lights and were going downstairs, when some question arose about the stuff of the frock, whatever it was. Mrs. Holder had mounted on a chair to look close at the stuff by the gaslight; and this was my bogey!

We had a delightful custom in nursery days, devised by my mother, that on festival occasions, such as birthdays or at Christmas, our presents were given us in the evening by a fairy called Abracadabra.

The first time the fairy appeared, we heard, after tea, in the hall, the hoarse notes of a horn. We rushed out in amazement. Down in the hall, talking to an aunt of mine who was staying in the house, stood a veritable fairy, in a scarlet dress, carrying a wand and a scarlet bag, and wearing a high pointed scarlet hat, of the shape of an extinguisher. My aunt called us down; and we saw that the fairy had the face of a great ape, dark-brown, spectacled, of a good-natured aspect, with a broad grin, and a curious crop of white hair, hanging down behind and on each side. Unfortunately my eldest brother, a very clever and imaginative child, was seized with a panic so insupportable at the sight of the face, that his present had to be given him hurriedly, and he was led away, blanched and shuddering, to the nursery. After that, the fairy never appeared except when he was at school: but long after, when I was looking in a lumber-room with my brother for some mislaid toys, I found in a box the mask of Abracadabra and the horn. I put it hurriedly on, and blew a blast on the horn, which seemed to be of tortoise-shell with metal fittings. To my amazement, he turned perfectly white, covered his face with his hands, and burst out with the most dreadful moans. I thought at first that he was making believe to be frightened, but I saw in a minute or two that he had quite lost control of himself, and the things were hurriedly put away. At the time I thought it a silly kind of affectation. But I perceive now that he had had a real shock the first time he had seen the mask; and though he was then a big schoolboy, the terror was indelible. Who can say of what old inheritance of fear that horror of the great ape-like countenance was the sign? He had no associations of fear with apes, but it must have been, I think, some dim old primeval terror, dating from some ancestral encounter with a forest monster. In no other way can I explain it.

Again, as a child, I was once sitting at dinner with my parents, reading an old bound-up *Saturday Magazine*, looking at the pictures, and waiting for dessert. I turned a page, and saw a picture of a Saint, lying on the ground, holding up a cross, and a huge and cloudy fiend with vast bat-like wings bending over him, preparing to clutch him, but deterred by the sacred emblem. That was a really terrible shock. I turned the page hastily, and said nothing, though it deprived me of speech and appetite. My father noticed my distress, and asked if I felt unwell, but I said "No." I got through dessert somehow; but then I had to say good-night, go out into the dimly-lit hall, slip the volume back into the bookcase, and get upstairs. I tore up the staircase, feeling the air full of wings and clutching hands. That was too bad ever to be spoken of; and as I did not remember which volume it was, I was never able to look at the set of magazines again for fear of encountering it; and strange to say some years afterwards, when I was an Eton boy, I looked curiously for the picture, and again experienced the same overwhelming horror.

My youngest brother, too, an imaginative child, could never be persuaded by any bribes or entreaties to go into a dark room to fetch anything out. Nothing would induce him. I remember that he was catechised at the tea-table as to what he expected to find, to which he replied at once, with a horror-stricken look and a long stammer, "B—b—b—bloodstained corpses!"

It seems fantastic and ridiculous enough to older people, but the horror of the dark and of the unknown which some children have is not a thing to be laughed at, nor should it be unsympathetically combated. One must remember that experience has not taught a child scepticism; he thinks that anything in the world may happen; and all the monsters of nursery tales, goblins, witches, evil fairies, dragons, which a child in daylight will know to be imaginary, begin, as the dusk draws on, to become appalling possibilities. They may be somewhere about, lurking in cellars and cupboards and lofts and dark entries by day, and at night they may slip out to do what harm they can. For children, not far from the gates of birth, are still strongly the victims of primeval and inherited fears, not corrected by the habitual current of life. It is not a reason for depriving children of the joys of the old tales and the exercise of the faculty of wonder; but the tendency should be very carefully guarded and watched, because these sudden shocks may make indelible marks, and leave a little weak spot in the mind which may prove difficult to heal.

It is not only these spectral terrors against which children have to be guarded. All severity and sharp indignity of punishment, all intemperate anger, all roughness of treatment, should be kept in strict restraint. There are noisy, boisterous, healthy children, of course, who do not resent or even dread sharp usage. But it is not always easy to discover the sensitive child, because fear of displeasure will freeze him into a stupor of apparent dullness and stubbornness. I am always infuriated by stupid people who regret the disappearance of sharp, stern, peremptory punishments, and lament the softness of the rising generation. If punishment must be inflicted, it should be done good-naturedly and robustly as a natural tit-for-tat. Anger should be reserved for things like spitefulness and dishonesty and cruelty. There is nothing more utterly confusing to the childish mind than to have trifling faults treated with wrath and indignation. It is true that, in the world of nature, punishment seems often wholly disproportionate to offences. Nature will penalise carelessness in a disastrous fashion, and spare the cautious and prudent sinner. But there is no excuse for us, if we have any sense of justice and patience at all, for not setting a better example. We ought to show children that there is a moral order which we are endeavouring to administer. If parents and schoolmasters, who are both judges and executioners, allow their own rule to be fortuitous, indulge their own irritable moods, punish severely a trifling fault, and sentimentalise or condone a serious one, a child is utterly confused. I know several people who have had their lives blighted, have been made suspicious, cynical, crafty, and timid, by severe usage and bullying and open contempt in childhood. The thing to avoid, for all who are responsible in the smallest degree for the nurture of children, is to call in the influence of fear; one may speak plainly of consequences, but even there one must not exaggerate, as schoolmasters often do, for the best of motives, about moral faults; one may punish deliberate and repeated disobedience, wanton cruelty, persistent and selfish disregard of the rights of others, but one must warn many times, and never try to triumph over a fault by the infliction of a shock of any kind. The shock is the most cruel and cowardly sort of punishment, and if we wilfully use it, then we are perpetuating the sad tyranny of instinctive fear, and using the strength of a great angel to do the work of a demon, such as I saw long ago in the old magazine, and felt its tyranny for many days.

As a child the one thing I was afraid of was the possibility of my father's displeasure. We did not see a great deal of him, because he was a much occupied headmaster; and he was to me a stately and majestic presence, before whom the whole created world seemed visibly to bow. But he was deeply anxious about our upbringing, and had a very strong sense of his responsibility; and he would sometimes reprove us rather sternly for some extremely trifling thing, the way one ate one's food, or spoke, or behaved. This descended upon me as a cloud of darkness; I attempted no excuses, I did not explain or defend myself; I simply was crushed and confounded. I do not think it was the right method. He never punished us, but we were not at ease with him. I remember the agony with which I heard a younger sister once repeat to him some silly and profane little jokes which a good-natured and absurd old lady had told us in the nursery. I felt sure he would disapprove, as he did. I knew quite well in my childish mind that it was harmless nonsense, and did not give us a taste for ungodly mirth. But I could not intervene or expostulate. I am sure that my father had not the slightest idea how weighty and dominant he was; but many of the things he rebuked would have been better not noticed, or if noticed only made fun of, while I feel that he ought to have given us more opportunity of stating our case. He simply frightened me into having a different morality when I was in his presence to what I had elsewhere. But he did not make me love goodness thereby, and only gave me a sense that certain things, harmless in themselves, must not be done or said in the presence of papa. He did not always remember his own rules, and there was thus an element of injustice in his rebukes, which one merely accepted as part of his awful and unaccountable greatness.

When I was transferred to a private school, a great big place, very well managed in every way, I lived for a time in atrocious terror of everything and everybody. I was conscious of a great code of rules which I did not know or understand, which I might quite unwittingly break, and the consequences of which might be fatal. I was never punished or caned, nor was I ever bullied. But I simply effaced myself as far as possible, and lived in dread of disaster. The thought even now of certain high blank walls with lofty barred windows, the remembered smells of certain passages and corners, the tall form and flashing eye of our headmaster and the faint fragrance of Havana cigars which hung about him, the bare corridors with their dark cupboards, the stone stairs and iron railings—all this gives me a far-off sense of dread. I can give no reason for my unhappiness there; but I can recollect waking in the early summer mornings, hearing the screams of peacocks from an adjoining garden, and thinking with a dreadful sense of isolation and despair at all the possibilities of disaster that lay hid in the day. I am sure it was not a wholesome experience. One need not fear the world more than is necessary—but my only dream of peace was the escape to the delights of home, and the thought of the larger world was only a thing that I shrank from and shuddered at.

No, it is wrong to say one had no friends, but how few they seemed and how clearly they stand out! I did not make friends among the boys; they were pleasant enough acquaintances, some of them, but not to be trusted or confided in; they had to be kept at arm's length, and one's real life guarded and hoarded away from them; because if one told them anything about one's home or one's ideas, it might be repeated, and the sacred facts shouted in one's ears as taunts and jests. But there was a little bluff master, a clergyman, with shaggy rippled red-brown hair and a face like a pug-dog. He was kind to me, and had me to lunch one Sunday in a villa out at Barnes—that was a breath of life, to sit in a homelike room and look at old *Punches* half the afternoon; and there was another young man, a master, rather stout and pale, with whom I shared some little jokes, and who treated me as he might treat a younger brother; he was pledged, I remember, to give me a cake if I won an Eton Scholarship, and royally he redeemed his promise. He died of heart disease a little while after I left the school. I had promised to write to him from Eton and never did so, and I had a little pang about that when I heard of his death. And then there was the kind handsome loud-voiced maid of my dormitory, Underwood by name, who was always just and kind, and who, even when she rated us, as she did at times, had always something human beckoning from her handsome eye. I can see her now, with her sleeves tucked up, and her big white muscular arms, washing a refractory little boy who fought shy of soap and water. I had a wild idea of giving her a kiss when I went away, and I think she would have liked that. She told me I had always been a good boy, and that she was sorry that I was going; but I did not dare to embrace her.

And then there was dear Louisa, the matron of the little sanatorium on the Mortlake road. She had been a former housemaid of ours; she was a strong sturdy woman, with a deep voice like a man; and when I arrived there ill—I was often ill in those days—she used to hug and kiss me and even cry over me; and the happiest days I spent at school were in that poky little house, reading in Louisa's little parlour, while she prepared some special dish as a treat for my supper; or sitting hour by hour at the window of my room upstairs, watching a grocer opposite set out his window. I certainly did love Louisa with all my heart; and it was almost pleasant to be ill, to be welcomed by her and petted and made much of. "My own dear boy," she used to say, and it was music in my ears.

I feel on looking back that, if I had children of my own, I should study very carefully to avoid any sort of terrorism. Psychologists tell us that the nervous shocks of early years are the things that leave indelible marks throughout life. I believe that mental specialists often make a careful study of the dreams of those whose minds are afflicted, because it is held that dreams very often continue to reproduce in later life the mental shocks of childhood. Anger, intemperate punishment, any attempt to produce instant submission and dismay in children, is very apt to hurt the nervous organisation. Of course it is easy enough to be careful about these things in sheltered environments, where there is some security and refinement of life. And this opens up a vast problem which cannot be touched on here, because it is practically certain that many children in poor and unsatisfactory homes sustain shocks to their mental organisation in early life which damage them irreparably, and which could be avoided if they could be brought up on more wholesome and tender lines.

VII

FEARS OF BOYHOOD

THERE is a tendency, I am sure, in books, to shirk the whole subject of fear, as though it were a thing disgraceful, shameful, almost unmentionable. The coward, the timid person, receives very little sympathy; he is rather like one tainted with a shocking disease, of which the less said the better. He is not viewed with any sympathy or commiseration, but as something almost lower in the scale of humanity. Take the literature that deals with school life, for instance. I do not think that there is any province of our literature so inept, so conventional, so entirely lacking in reality, as the books which deal with the life of schools. The difficulty of writing them is very great, because they can only be reconstructed by an effort of memory. The boy himself is quite unable to give expression to his thoughts and feelings; school life is a time of sharp, eager, often rather savage emotions, lived by beings who have no sense of proportion, no knowledge of life, no idea of what is really going on in the world. The actual incidents which occur are very trivial, and yet to the fresh minds and spirits of boyhood they seem all charged with an intense significance. Then again the talk of schoolboys is wholly immature and shapeless. They cannot express themselves, and moreover there is a very strict and peremptory convention which dictates what may be talked about and what may not. No society in the world is under so oppressive a taboo. They must not speak of anything emotional or intellectual, at the cost of being thought a fool or a prig. They talk about games, they gossip about boys and masters, sometimes their conversation is nasty and bestial. But it conceals very real if very fitful emotions; yet it is impossible to recall or to reconstruct; and when older people attempt to reconstruct it, they remember the emotions which underlay it, and the eager interests out of which it all sprang; and they make it something picturesque, epigrammatic, and vernacular which is wholly untrue to life. The fact is that the talk of schoolboys is very trivial and almost wholly symbolical; emotion reveals itself in glance and gesture, not in word at all. I suppose that most of us remember our boyish friendships, ardent and eager personal admirations, extraordinary deifications of quite commonplace boys, emotions none of which were ever put into words at all, hardly even into coherent thought, and were yet a swift and vital current of the soul.

Now the most unreal part of the reconstructions of school life is the insistence on the boyish code of honour. Neither as a boy nor as a schoolmaster did I ever have much evidence of this. There were certain hard and fast rules of conduct, like the rule which prevented any boy from giving information to a master against another boy. But this was not a conscientious thing. It was part of the tradition, and the social ostracism which was the penalty of its infraction was too severe to risk incurring. But the boys who cut a schoolfellow for telling tales, did not do it from any high-minded sense of violated honour.

It was simply a piece of self-defence, and the basis of the convention was merely this, that, if the rule were broken, it would produce an impossible sense of insecurity and peril. However much boys might on the whole approve of, respect, and even like their masters, still they could not make common cause with them. The school was a perfectly definite community, inside of which it was often convenient and pleasant to do things which would be penalised if discovered; and thus the whole stability of that society depended upon a certain secrecy. The masters were not disliked for finding out the infractions of rules, if only such infractions were patent and obvious. A master who looked too closely into things, who practised any sort of espionage, who tried to extort confession, was disapproved of as a menace, and it was convenient to label him a sneak and a spy, and to say that he did not play the game fair. But all this was a mere tradition. Boys do not reflect much, or look into the reasons of things. It does not occur to them to credit masters with the motive of wishing to protect them against themselves, to minimise temptation, to shelter them from undesirable influences; that perhaps dawns on the minds of sensible and high-minded prefects, but the ordinary boy just regards the master as an opposing power, whom he hoodwinks if he can.

And then the boyish ideal of courage is a very incomplete one. He does not recognise it as courage if a sensitive, conscientious, and right-minded boy risks unpopularity by telling a master of some evil practice which is spreading in a school. He simply regards it as a desire to meddle, a priggish and pragmatical act, and even as a sneaking desire to inflict punishment by proxy.

Courage, for the schoolboy, is merely physical courage, aplomb, boldness, recklessness, high-handedness. The hero of school life is one like Odysseus, who is strong, inventive, daring, full of resource. The point is to come out on the top. Odysseus yields to sensual delight, he is cruel, vindictive, and incredibly deceitful. It is evident that successful beguiling, the power of telling an elaborate, plausible, and imperturbable lie on occasions, is an heroic quality in the *Odyssey*. Odysseus is not a man who scorns to deceive, or who would rather take the consequences than utter a falsehood. His strength rather lies in his power, when at bay, of flashing into some monstrous fiction, dramatising the situation, playing an adopted part, with confidence and assurance. One sees traces of the same thing in the Bible. The story of Jacob deceiving Isaac, and pretending to be Esau in order to secure a blessing is not related with disapprobation. Jacob does not forfeit his blessing when his deceit is discovered. The whole incident is regarded rather as a master-stroke of cunning and inventiveness. Esau is angry not because Jacob has employed such trickery, but because he has succeeded in supplanting him.

I remember, as a boy at Eton, seeing a scene which left a deep impression on me. There was a big unpleasant unscrupulous boy of great physical strength, who was a noted football player. He was extremely unpopular in the school, because he was rude, sulky, and overbearing, and still more because he took unfair advantages in games. There was a hotly contested house-match, in which he tried again and again to evade rules, while he was for ever appealing to the umpires against violations of rule by the opposite side. His own house was ultimately victorious, but feeling ran very high indeed, because it was thought that the victory was unfairly won. The crowd of boys who had been watching the match drifted away in a state of great exasperation, and finally collected in front of the house of the unpopular player, hissed and hooted him. He took very little notice of the demonstration and walked in, when there arose a babel of howls. He turned round and came out again, facing the crowd. I can see him now, all splashed and muddy, with his shirt open at the neck. He was pale, ugly, and sinister; but he surveyed us all with entire effrontery, drew out a pince-nez, being very short-sighted, and then looked calmly round as if surprised. I have certainly never seen such an exhibition of courage in my life. He knew that he had not a single friend present, and he did not know that he would not be maltreated—there were indications of a rush being made. He did not look in the least picturesque; he was ugly, scowling, offensive. But he did not care a rap, and if he had been attacked, he would have defended himself with a will. It did not occur to me then, nor did it, I think, occur to anyone else, what an amazing bit of physical and moral courage it was. No one, then or after, had the slightest feeling of admiration for his pluck. "Did you ever see such a brute as P—— looked?" was the only sort of comment made.

This just serves to illustrate my point, that boys have no real discernment for what is courageous. What they admire is a certain grace and spirit, and the hero is not one who constrains himself to do an unpopular thing from a sense of duty, not even the boy who, being unpopular like P——, does a satanically brave thing. Boys have no admiration for the boy who defies *them;* what they like to see is the defiance of a common foe. They admire gallant, modest, spirited, picturesque behaviour, not the dull and faithful obedience to the sense of right.

Of course things have altered for the better. Masters are no longer stern, severe, abrupt, formidable, unreasonable. They know that many a boy, who would be inclined on the whole to tell the truth, can easily be frightened into telling a lie; but they have not yet contrived to put the sense of honour among boys in the right proportion. Such stories as that of George Washington—when the children were asked who had cut down the apple-tree, and he rose and said, "Sir, I cannot tell a lie; it was I who did it with my little hatchet"—do not really take the imagination of boys captive. How constantly did worthy preachers at Eton tell the story of how Bishop Selwyn, às a boy, rose and left the room at a boat-supper because an improper song was sung! That anecdote was regarded with undisguised amusement, and it was simply thought to be a piece of priggishness. I cannot imagine that any boy ever heard the story and went away with a glowing desire to do likewise. The incident really belongs to the domain of manners rather than to that of morals.

The truth is really that boys at school have a code which resembles that of the old chivalry. The hero may be sensual, unscrupulous, cruel, selfish, indifferent to the welfare of others. But if he bears himself gallantly, if he has a charm of look and manner, if he is a deft performer in the prescribed athletics, he is the object of profound and devoted admiration. It is really physical courage, skill, prowess, personal attractiveness which is envied and praised. A dull, heavy, painstaking, conscientious boy with a sturdy sense of duty may be respected, but he is not followed; while the imaginative, sensitive, nervous, highly-strung boy, who may have the finest qualities of all within him, is apt to be the most despised. Such a boy is often no good at games, because public performance disconcerts him; he cannot make a ready answer, he has no aplomb, no cheek, no smartness; and he is consequently thought very little of.

To what extent this sort of instinctive preference can be altered, I do not know; it certainly cannot be altered by sermons, and still less by edicts. Old Dr. Keate said, when he was addressing the school on the subject of fighting, "I must say that I like to see a boy return a blow!" It seems, if one considers it, to be a curious ideal to start life with, considering how little opportunity civilisation now gives for returning blows! Boys in fact are still educated under a system which seems to anticipate a combative and disturbed sort of life to follow, in which strength and agility, violence and physical activity, will have a value. Yet, as a matter of fact, such things have very little substantial value in an ordinary citizen's life at all, except in so far as they play their part in the elaborate cult of athletic exercises, with which we beguile the instinct which craves for manual toil. All the races, and games, and athletics cultivated so assiduously at school seem now to have very little aim in view. It is not important for ordinary life to be able to run a hundred yards, or even three miles, faster than another man; the judgment, the quickness of eye, the strength and swiftness of muscle needed to make a man a good batsman were all well enough in days when a man's life might afterwards depend on his use of sword and battle-axe. But now it only enables him to play games rather longer than other people, and to a certain extent ministers to bodily health, although the statistics of rowing would seem clearly to prove that it is a pursuit which is rather more apt to damage the vitality of strong boys than to increase the vitality of weak ones.

So, if we look facts fairly in the face, we see that much of the training of school life, especially in the direction of athletics, is really little more than the maintenance of a thoughtless old tradition, and that it is all directed to increase our admiration of prowess and grace and gallantry, rather than to fortify us in usefulness and manual skill and soundness of body. A boy at school may be a skilful carver or carpenter; he may have a real gift for engineering or mechanics; he may even be a good rider, a first-rate fisherman, an excellent shot. He may have good intellectual abilities, a strong memory, a power of expression; he may be a sound mathematician, a competent scientist; he may have all sorts of excellent moral qualities, be reliable, accurate, truthful, punctual, duty-loving; he may in fact be equipped for life and citizenship, able to play his part sturdily and manfully, and to do the world good service; but yet he may never win the smallest recognition or admiration in his school-days, while all the glory and honour and credit is still reserved for the graceful, attractive, high-spirited athlete, who may have nothing else in the background.

That is certainly the ideal of the boy, and the disconcerting thing is that it is also the ideal, practically if not theoretically, of the parent and the schoolmaster. The school still reserves all its best gifts, its sunshine and smiles, for the knightly and the skilful; it rewards all the qualities that are their own reward. Why, if it wishes to get the right scale adopted, does it not reward the thing which it professes to uphold as its best result, worth of character namely? It claims to be a training-ground for character first, but it does little to encourage secret and unobtrusive virtues. That is, it adds its prizes to the things which the natural man values, and it neglects to crown the one thing at which it professes first to aim. In doing this it only endorses the verdict of the world, and while it praises moral effort, it rewards success.

The issue of all this is that the sort of courage which it enforces is essentially a graceful and showy sort of courage, a lively readiness, a high-hearted fearlessness—so that timidity and slowness and diffidence and unreadiness become base and feeble qualities, when they are not the things of which anyone need be ashamed! Let me say then that moral courage, the patient and unrecognised facing of difficulties, the disregard of popular standards, solidity and steadfastness of purpose, the tranquil performance of tiresome and disagreeable duties, homely perseverance, are not the things which are regarded as supreme in the ideal of the school; so that the fear which is the shadow of sensitive and imaginative natures is turned into the wrong channels, and becomes a mere dread of doing the unpopular and unimpressive thing, or a craven determination not to be found out. And the dread of being obscure and unacceptable is what haunts the minds of boys brought up on these ambitious and competitive lines, rather than the fear which is the beginning of wisdom.

VIII

FEARS OF YOUTH

THE fears of youth are as a rule just the terrors of self-consciousness and shyness. They are a very irrational thing, something purely instinctive and of old inheritance. How irrational they are is best proved by the fact that shyness is caused mostly by the presence of strangers; there are many young people who are bashful, awkward, and tongue-tied in the presence of strangers, whose tremors wholly disappear in the family circle. If these were rational fears, they might be caused by the consciousness of the inspection and possible disapproval of those among whom one lives, and whose annoyance and criticism might have unpleasant practical effects. Yet they are caused often by the presence of those whose disapproval is not of the smallest consequence, those, in fact, whom one is not likely to see again. One must look then for the cause of this, not in the fact that one's awkwardness and inefficiency is likely to be blamed by those of one's own circle, but simply in the terror of the unknown and the unfamiliar. It is probably therefore an old inherited instinct, coming from a time when the sight of a stranger might contain in it a menace of some hostile usage. If one questions a shy boy or girl as to what it is they are afraid of in the presence of strangers, they are quite unable to answer. They are not afraid of anything that will be said or done; and yet they will have become intensely conscious of their own appearance and movements and dress, and will be quite unable to command themselves. That it is a thing which can be easily cured is obvious from the fact which I often observed when I was a schoolmaster, that as a rule the boys who came from houses where there was much entertaining, and a constant coming and going of guests, very rarely suffered from such shyness. They had got used to the fact that strangers could be depended upon to be kind and friendly, and instead of looking upon a new person as a possible foe, they regarded him as a probable friend.

I often think that parents do not take enough trouble in this respect to make children used to strangers. What often happens is that parents are themselves shy and embarrassed in the presence of strangers, and when they notice that their children suffer from the same awkwardness, they criticise them afterwards, partly because they are vexed at their own clumsy performance; and thus the shyness is increased, because the child, in addition to his sense of shyness before strangers, has in the background of his mind the feeling that any *mauvaise honte* that he may display may be commented upon afterwards. No exhibition of shyness on the part of a boy or girl should ever be adverted upon by parents. They should take for granted that no one is ever willingly shy, and that it is a misery which all would avoid if they could. It is even better to allow children considerable freedom of speech with strangers, than to repress and silence them. Of course impertinence and unpleasant comments, such as children will sometimes make on the appearance or manners of strangers, must be checked, but it should be on the grounds of the unpleasantness of such remarks, and not on the ground of forwardness. On the other hand, all attempts on the part of a child to be friendly and courteous to strangers should be noted and praised; a child should be encouraged to look upon itself as an integral part of a circle, and not as a silent and lumpish auditor.

Probably too there are certain physical and psychological laws, which we do not at all understand, which account for the curious subjective effects which certain people have at close quarters; there is something hypnotic and mesmeric about the glance of certain eyes; and there is in all probability a curious blending of mental currents in an assembly of people, which is not a mere fancy, but a very real physical fact. Personalities radiate very real and unmistakable influences, and probably the undercurrent of thought which happens to be in one's mind when one is with others has an effect, even if one says or does nothing to indicate one's preoccupation. A certain amount of this comes from an unconscious inference on the part of the recipients. We often augur, without any very definite rational process, from the facial expressions, gestures, movements, tones of others, what their frame of mind is. But I believe that there is a great deal more than that. We must all know that when we are with friends to whose moods and emotions we are attuned, there takes place a singular degree of thought-transference, quite apart from speech. I had once a great friend with whom I was accustomed to spend much time *tête-à-tête*. We used to travel together and spend long periods, day after day, in close conjunction, often indeed sharing the same bedroom. It became a matter at first of amusement and interest, but afterwards an accepted fact, that we could often realise, even after a long silence, in what direction the other's thought was travelling. "How did you guess I was thinking of that?" would be asked. To which the reply was, "I did not guess—I knew." On the other hand I have an old and familiar friend, whom I know well and regard with great affection, but whose presence, and particularly a certain fixity of glance, often, even now, causes me a curious subjective disturbance which is not wholly pleasant, a sense of some odd psychical control which is not entirely agreeable.

I have another friend who is the most delightful and easy company in the world when we are alone together; but he is a sensitive and highly-strung creature, much affected by personal influences, and when I meet him in the company of other people he is often almost unrecognisable. His mind becomes critical, combative, acrid; he does not say what he means, he is touched by a vague excitement, and there passes over him an unnatural sort of brilliance, of a hard and futile kind, which makes him sacrifice consideration and friendliness to the instinctive desire to produce an effect and to score a point. I sometimes actually detest him when he is one of a circle. I feel inclined to say to him, "If only you could let your real self appear, and drop this tiresome posturing and fencing, you would be as delightful as you are to me when I am alone with you; but this hectic tittering and feverish jocosity is not only not your real self, but it gives others an impression of a totally unreal and not very agreeable person." But, alas, this is just the sort of thing one cannot say to a friend!

As one goes on in life, this terrible and disconcerting shyness of youth disappears. We begin to realise, with a wholesome loss of vanity and conceit, how very little people care or even notice how we are dressed, how we look, what we say. We learn that other people are as much preoccupied with their thoughts and fancies and reflections as we are with our own. We realise that if we are anxious to produce an agreeable impression, we do so far more by being interested and sympathetic, than by attempting a brilliance which we cannot command. We perceive that other people are not particularly interested in our crude views, nor very grateful for the expression of them. We acquire the power of combination and co-operation, in losing the desire for splendour and domination. We see that people value ease and security, more than they admire originality and fantastic contradiction. And so we come to the blessed time when, instead of reflecting after a social occasion whether we did ourselves justice, we begin to consider rather the impression we have formed of other personalities.

I believe that we ought to have recourse to very homely remedies indeed for combating shyness. It is of no use to try to console and distract ourselves with lofty thoughts, and to try to keep eternity and the hopes of man in mind. We so become only more self-conscious and superior than ever. The fact remains that the shyness of youth causes agonies both of anticipation and retrospect; if one really wishes to get rid of it, the only way is to determine to get used somehow to society, and not to endeavour to avoid it; and as a practical rule to make up one's mind, if possible, to ask people questions, rather than to meditate impressive answers. Asking other people questions about things to which they are likely to know the answers is one of the shortest cuts to popularity and esteem. It is wonderful to reflect how much distress personal bashfulness causes people, how much they would give to be rid of it, and yet how very little trouble they ever take to acquiring any method of dealing with the difficulty. I see a good deal of undergraduates, and am often aware that they are friendly and responsive, but without any power of giving expression to it. I sometimes see them suffering acutely from shyness before my eyes. But a young man who can bring himself to ask a perfectly simple question about some small matter of common interest is comparatively rare; and yet it is generally the simplest way out of the difficulty.

IX

FEARS OF MIDDLE AGE

Now with all the tremors, reactions, glooms, shadows, and despairs of youth—it is easy enough to forget them, but they were there—goes a power of lifting and lighting up in a moment at a chord of music, a glance, a word, the song of a bird, the scent of a flower, a flying sunburst, which fills life up like a cup with bubbling and sparkling liquor.

> "My soul, be patient! Thou shalt find
> A litle matter mend all this!"

And that is the part of youth which we remember, till on looking back it seems like a time of wandering with like-hearted comrades down some sweet-scented avenue of golden sun and green shade. Our memory plays us beautifully false—*splendide mendax*—till one wishes sometimes that old and wise men, re-telling the story of their life, could recall for the comfort of youth some part of its languors and mischances, its bitter jealousies, its intense and poignant sense of failure.

And then in a moment the door of life opens. One day I was an irresponsible pleasure-loving, fantastic youth, and a week later I was, or it seemed to me that I was, a professional man with all the cares of a pedagogue upon my back. It filled me at first, I remember, with a gleeful amazement, to find myself in the desk, holding forth, instead of on the form listening. It seemed delicious at first to have the power of correcting and slashing exercises, and placing boys in order, instead of being corrected and examined, and competing for a place. It was a solemn game at the outset. Then came the other side of the picture. One's pupils were troublesome, they did badly in examinations, they failed unaccountably; and one had a glimpse too of some of the tragedies of school life. Almost insensibly I became aware that I had a task to perform, that my mistakes involved boys in disaster, that I had the anxious care of other destinies; and thus, almost before I knew it, came a new cloud on the horizon, the cloud of anxiety. I could not help seeing that I had mismanaged this boy and misdirected that; that one could not treat them as ingenuous and lively playthings, but that what one said and did set a mark which perhaps could not be effaced. Gradually other doubts and problems made themselves felt. I had to administer a system of education in which I did not wholly believe; I saw little by little that the rigid old system of education was a machine which, if it made a highly accomplished product out of the best material, wasted an enormous amount of boyish interest and liveliness, and stultified the feebler sort of mind. Then came the care of a boarding-house, close relations with parents, a more real knowledge of the infinite levity of boy nature. I became mixed up with the politics of the place, the chance of more ambitious positions floated before me; the need for tact, discretion, judiciousness, moderation, tolerance emphasized itself. I am here outlining my own experience, but it is only one of many similar experiences. I became a citizen without knowing it, and my place in the world, my status, success, all became definite things which I had to secure.

The cares, the fears, the anxieties of middle life lie for most men and women in this region; if people are healthy and active, they generally arrive at a considerable degree of equanimity; they do not anticipate evil, and they take the problems of life cheerfully enough as they come; but yet come they do, and too many men and women are tempted to throw overboard scornfully and disdainfully the dreams of youth as a luxury which they cannot afford to indulge, and to immerse themselves in practical cares, month after month, with perhaps the hope of a fairly careless and idle holiday at intervals. What I think tends to counteract this for many people is love and marriage, the wonder and amazement of having children of their own, and all the offices of tenderness that grow up naturally beside their path. But this again brings a whole host of fears and anxieties as well—arrangements, ways and means, household cares, illnesses, the homely stuff of life, much of it enjoyed, much of it cheerfully borne, and often very bravely and gallantly endured. It is out of this simple material that life has to be constructed. But there is a twofold danger in all this. There is a danger of cynicism, the frame of mind in which a man comes to face little worries as one might put up an umbrella in a shower—"Thou know'st 'tis common!" Out of that grows up a rude dreariness, a philosophy which has nothing dignified about it, but is merely a recognition of the fact that life is a poor affair, and that one cannot hope to have things to one's mind. Or there is a dull frame of mind which implies a meek resignation, a sense of disappointment about life, borne with a mournful patience, a sense of one's sphere having somehow fallen short of one's deserts. This produces the grumpy paterfamilias who drowses over a paper or grumbles over a pipe; such a man is inimitably depicted by Mr. Wells in *Marriage*. That sort of ugly disillusionment, that publicity of disappointment, that frank disregard of all concerns except one's own, is one of the most hideous features of middle-class life, and it is rather characteristically English. It sometimes conceals a robust good sense and even kindliness; but it is a base thing at best, and seems to be the shadow of commercial prosperity. Yet it at least implies a certain sturdiness of character, and a stubborn belief in one's own merits which is quite impervious to the lessons of experience. On sensitive and imaginative people the result of the professional struggle with life, the essence of which is often social pretentiousness, is different. It ends in a mournful and distracted kind of fatigue, a tired sort of padding along after life, a timid bewilderment at conditions which one cannot alter, and which yet have no dignity or seemliness.

What is there that is wrong with all this? The cause is easy enough to analyse. It is the result of a system which develops conventional, short-sighted, complicated households, averse to effort, fond of pleasure, and with tastes which are expensive without being refined. The only cure would seem to be that men and women should be born different, with simple active generous natures; it is easy to say that! But the worst of the situation is that the sordid banality and ugly tragedy of their lot do not dawn on the people concerned. Greedy vanity in the more robust, lack of moral courage and firmness in the more sensitive, with a social organisation that aims at a surface dignity and a cheap showiness, are the ingredients of this devil's cauldron. The worst of it is that it has no fine elements at all. There is a nobility about real tragedy which evokes a quality of passionate and sincere emotion. There is something essentially exalted about a fierce resistance, a desperate failure. But this abject, listless dreariness, which can hardly be altered or expressed, this miserable floating down the muddy current, where there is no sharp repentance or fiery battling, nothing but a mean abandonment to a meaningless and unintelligible destiny, seems to have in it no seed of recovery at all.

The dark shadow of professional anxiety is that it has no tragic quality; it is like ploughing on day by day through endless mud-flats. One does not feel, in the presence of sharp suffering or bitter loss, that they ought not to exist. They are there, stern, implacable, august; stately enemies, great combatants. There is a significance about their very awfulness. One may fall before them, but they pass like a great express train, roaring, flashing, things deliberately and intently designed; but these dull failures which seem not the outgrowth of anyone's fierce longing or wilful passion, but of everyone's laziness and greediness and stupidity, how is one to face them? It is the helpless death of the quagmire, not the death of the fight or the mountain-top. Is there, we ask ourselves, anything in the mind of God which corresponds to comfort-loving vulgarity, if so strong and yet so stagnant a stream can overflow the world? The bourgeois ideal! One would rather have tyranny or savagery than anything so gross and smug.

And yet we see high-spirited and ardent husbands drawn into this by obstinate and vulgar-minded wives. We see fine-natured and sensitive women engulfed in it by selfish and ambitious husbands. The tendency is awfully and horribly strong, and it wins, not by open combat, but by secret and dull persistence. And one sees too—I have seen it many times—children of delicate and eager natures, who would have flourished and expanded in more generous air, become conventional and commonplace and petty, concerned about knowing the right people and doing the right things, and making the same stupid and paltry show, which deceives no one.

There is nothing for it but independence and simplicity and, perhaps best of all, a love of beauty. William Morris asserted passionately enough that art was the only cure for all this dreariness—the love of beautiful sounds and sights and words; and I think that is true, if it be further extended to a perception of the quality of beauty in the conduct and relations of life. For those are the cheap and reasonable pleasures of life, accessible to all; and if men and women cared for work first and the decent simplicities of wholesome living, and could further find their pleasure in art, in whatever form, then I believe that many of these fears and anxieties, so maiming and impairing to all that is fine in life, would vanish quietly out of being. The thing seems both beautiful and possible, because one knows of households where it is so, and where it grows up naturally and easily enough. I know households of both kinds—where on the one hand the standard is ambitious and mean, where the inmates calculate everything with a view to success, or rather to producing an impression of success; and there all talk and intercourse is an unreal thing, not the outflow of natural interests and pleasant tastes, but a sham culture and a refinement that is only pursued because it is the right sort of surface to present to the world. One submits to it with boredom, one leaves it with relief. They have got the right people together, they have shown that they can command their attendance; it is all ceremony and waste.

And then I know households where one sees in the books, the pictures, the glances, the gestures, the movements of the inmates, a sort of grace and delicacy which comes of really caring about things that are beautiful and fine. Sincere things are simply said, humour bubbles up and breaks in laughter; one feels that light is thrown on a hundred topics and facts and personalities. The whole of life then becomes a garden teeming with strange and wonderful secrets, and influences that flash and radiate, passing on into some mysterious and fragrant gloom.

Everything there seems charged with significance and charm; there are no pretences—there are preferences, prejudices if you will; but there is tolerance and sympathy, and a desire to see the point of view of others. The effect of such an atmosphere is to set one wondering how one has contrived to miss the sense of so much that is beautiful and interesting in life, and sends one away longing to perceive more, and determined if possible to interpret life more truly and more graciously.

X

FEARS OF AGE

And then age creeps on ; and that brings fears of its own, and fears that are all the more intolerable because they are not definite fears at all, merely a loss of nervous vigour, which attaches itself to the most trivial detail and magnifies it into an insuperable difficulty. A friend of mine who was growing old once confided to me that foreign travel, which used to be such a delight to him, was now getting burdensome. "It is all right when I have once started," he said, "but for days before I am the prey of all kinds of apprehensions." "What sort of apprehensions?" I said. He laughed, and replied, "Well, it is almost too absurd to mention, but I find myself oppressed with anxiety for weeks beforehand as to whether, when we get to Calais, we shall find places in the train." And I remember, too, how a woman friend of mine once told me that she called at the house of an elderly couple in London, people of rank and wealth. Their daughter met her in the drawing-room and said, "I am glad you are come—you may be able to cheer my mother up. We are going down to-morrow to our place in the country; the servants and the luggage went this morning, and my mother and father are to drive down this afternoon—my mother is very low about it." "What is the matter?" said my friend. The daughter replied, "She is afraid that they will not get there in time!" "In time for what?" said my friend, thinking that there was some important engagement. "In time for tea!" said the daughter gravely.

It is all very well to laugh at such fears, but they are not natural fears at all, they just indicate a low vitality; they are the symptoms and not the causes of a disease. It is the frame of mind of the sluggard in the Bible who says, "There is a lion in the way." Younger people are apt to be irritated by what seems a wilful creating of apprehensions. They ought rather to be patient and reassuring, and compassionate to the weakness of nerve for which it stands.

With such fears as these may be classed all the unreal but none the less distressing fears about health which beset people all their lives, in some cases; it is extremely annoying to healthy people to find a man reduced to depression and silence at the possibility of taking cold, or at the fear of having eaten something unwholesome. I remember an elderly gentleman who had lived a vigorous and unselfish life, and was indeed a man of force and character, whose activity was entirely suspended in later years by his fear of catching cold or of over-tiring himself. He was a country clergyman, and used to spend the whole of Sunday between his services, in solitary seclusion, "resting," and retire to bed the moment the evening service was over; moreover his dread of taking cold was such that he invariably wore a hat in the winter months to go from the drawing-room to the dining-room for dinner, even if there were guests in his house. He used to jest about it, and say that it no doubt must look curious; but he added that he had found it a wise precaution, and that we had no idea how disabling his colds were. Even a very healthy friend of my own standing has told me that if he ever lies awake at night he is apt to exaggerate the smallest and most trifling sense of discomfort into the symptom of some dangerous disease. Let me quote the well-known case of Hans Andersen, whose imagination was morbidly strong. He found one morning when he awoke that he had a small pimple under his left eyebrow. He reflected with distress upon the circumstance, and soon came to the rueful conclusion that the pimple would probably increase in size, and deprive him of the sight of his left eye. A friend calling upon him in the course of the morning found him writing, in a mood of solemn resignation, with one hand over the eye in question, "practising," as he said, "how to read and write with the only eye that would soon be left him."

One's first impulse is to treat these self-inflicted sufferings as ridiculous and almost idiotic. But they are quite apt to beset people of effectiveness and ability. To call them irrational does not cure them, because they lie deeper than any rational process, and are in fact the superficial symptoms of some deep-seated weakness of nerve, while their very absurdity, and the fact that the mind cannot throw them off, only proves how strong they are. They are in fact signs of some profound uneasiness of mind; and the rational brain of such people, casting about for some reason to explain the fear with which they are haunted, fixes on some detail which is not worthy of serious notice. It is of course a species of local insanity and monomania, but it does not imply any general obscuration of faculties at all. Some of the most intellectual people are most at the mercy of such trials, and indeed they are rather characteristic of men and women whose brain is apt to work at high pressure. One recollects in the life of Shelley, how he used to be haunted by these insupportable fears. He was at one time persuaded that he had contracted leprosy, and he used to disconcert his acquaintances by examining solicitously their wrists and necks to see if he could detect symptoms of the same disease.

There is very little doubt that as medical knowledge progresses we shall know more about the cause of such hallucinations. To call them unreal is mere stupidity. Sensible people who suffer from them are often perfectly well aware of their unreality, and are profoundly humiliated by them. They are some disease or weakness of the imaginative faculty; and a friend of mine who suffered from such things told me that it was extraordinary to him to perceive the incredible ingenuity with which his brain under such circumstances used to find confirmation for his fears from all sorts of trivial incidents which at other times passed quite unnoticed. It is generally quite useless to think of removing the fear by combating the particular fancy; the affected centre, whatever it is, only turns feverishly to some other similar anxiety. Occupation of a quiet kind, exercise, rest, are the best medicine.

Sometimes these anxieties take a different form, and betray themselves by suspicion of other people's conduct and motives. That is of course allied to insanity. In sane and sound health we realise that we are not, as a rule, the objects of the malignity and spitefulness of others. We are perhaps obstacles to the carrying out of other people's plans; but men and women as a rule mind their own business, and are not much concerned to intervene in the designs and activities of others. Yet a man whose mental equilibrium is unstable is apt to think that if he is disappointed or thwarted it is the result of a deliberate conspiracy on the part of other people. If he is a writer, he thinks that other writers are aware of his merits, but are determined to .prevent them being recognised out of sheer ill-will. A man in robust health realises that he gets quite as much credit or even more credit than he deserves, and that his claims to attention are generously recognised; one has exactly as much influence and weight as one can get, and other people as a rule are much too much occupied in their own concerns to have either the time or the inclination to interfere. But as a man grows older, as his work stiffens and weakens, he falls out of the race, and he must be content to do so; and he is well advised if he puts his failure down to his own deficiencies, and not to the malice of others. The world is really very much on the look out for anything which amuses, delights, impresses, moves, or helps it; it is quick and generous in recognition of originality and force; and if a writer, as he gets older, finds his books neglected and his opinions disdained, he may be fairly sure that he has said his say, and that men are preoccupied with new ideas and new personalities. Of course this is a melancholy and disconcerting business, especially if one has been more concerned with personal prominence than with the worth and weight of one's ideas; mortified vanity is a sore trial. I remember once meeting an old author who, some thirty years before the date at which I met him, had produced a book which attracted an extraordinary amount of attention, though it has long since been forgotten. The old man had all the airs of solemn greatness, and I have seldom seen a more rueful spectacle than when a young and rising author was introduced to him, and when it became obvious that the young man had not only never heard of the old writer, but did not know the name of his book.

The question is what we can do to avoid falling under the dominion of these uncanny fears and fancies, as we fall from middle age to age. A dreary, dispirited, unhappy, peevish old man or old woman is a very miserable spectacle; while, at the same time, generous, courteous, patient, modest, tender old age is one of the most beautiful things in the world. We may of course resolve not to carry our dreariness into all circles, and if we find life a poor and dejected business, we can determine that we will not enlarge upon the theme. But the worst of discouragement is that it removes even the desire to play a part, or to make the most and best of ourselves. Like Mrs. Gummidge in *David Copperfield*, if we are reminded that other people have their troubles, we are apt to reply that we feel them more. One does not desire that people should unduly indulge themselves in self-dramatisation. There is something very repugnant in an elderly person who is bent on proving his importance and dignity, in laying claim to force and influence, in affecting to play a large part in the world. But there is something even more afflicting in the people who drop all decent pretence of dignity, and pour the product of an acrid and disappointed spirit into all conversations.

Age can establish itself very firmly in the hearts of its circle, if it is kind, sympathetic, appreciative, ready to receive confidences, willing to encourage the fitful despondencies of youth. But here again we are met by the perennial difficulty as to how far we can force ourselves to do things which we do not really want to do, and how far again, if we succeed in forcing ourselves into action, we can give any accent of sincerity and genuineness to our comments and questions.

In this particular matter, that of sympathy, a very little effort does undoubtedly go a long way, because there are a great many people in the world eagerly on the look out for any sign of sympathy, and not apt to scrutinise too closely the character of the sympathy offered. And the best part of having once forced oneself to exhibit sympathy, at whatever cost of strain and effort, is that one is at least ashamed to withdraw it.

I remember a foolish woman who was very anxious to retain the hold upon the active world which she had once possessed. She very seldom spoke of any subject but herself, her performances, her activities, the pressure of the claims which she was forced to try to satisfy. I can recall her now, with her sanguine complexion, her high voice, her anxious and restless eye wandering in search of admiration. "The day's post!" she cried, "that is one of my worst trials—so many duties to fulfil, so many requests for help, so many irresistible claims come before me in the pile of letters—that high," indicating about a foot and a half of linear measurement above the table. "It is the same story every day—a score of people bringing their little mugs of egotism to be filled at my pump of sympathy!"

It was a ridiculous exhibition, because one was practically sure that there was nothing of the kind going on. One was inclined to believe that they were mugs of sympathy filled at the pump of egotism! But if the thing were really being done, it was certainly worth doing!

One of the causes of the failure of nerve-force in age, which lies behind so much of these miseries, is that people who have lived at all active lives cannot bring themselves to realise their loss of vigour, and try to prolong the natural energies of middle age into the twilight of elderliness. Men and women cling to activities, not because they enjoy them, but to delude themselves into believing that they are still young. That terrible inability to resign positions, the duties of which one cannot adequately fulfil, which seems so disgraceful and unconscientious a handling of life to the young, is often a pathetic clinging to youth. Such veterans do not reflect that the only effect of such tenacity is partly that other people do their work, and partly also that the critic observes that if a post can be adequately filled by so old a man it is a proof that such a post ought not to exist. The tendency ought to be met as far as possible by fixing age-limits to all positions. Because even if the old and weary do consult their friends as to the advisability of retirement, it is very hard for the friends cordially to recommend it. A public man once told me that a very aged official consulted him as to the propriety of resignation. He said in his reply something complimentary about the value of the veteran's services. Whereupon the old man replied that as he set so high an estimation upon his work, he would endeavour to hold on a little longer!

The conscientious thing to do, as we get older and find ourselves slower, more timid, more inactive, more anxious, is to consult a candid friend, and to follow his advice rather than our own inclination; a certain fearfulness, an avoidance of unpleasant duty, a dreary foreboding, is apt to be characteristic of age. But we must meet it philosophically. We must reflect that we have done our work, and that an attempt to galvanise ourselves into activity is sure to result in depression. So we must condense our energies, be content to play a little, to drowse a little, to watch with interest the game of life in which we cannot take a hand, until death falls as naturally upon our wearied eyes as sleep falls upon the eyes of a child tired with a long summer day of eager pleasure and delight.

But there is one practical counsel that may here be given to all who find a tendency to dread and anxiety creeping upon them as life advances. I have known very truly and deeply religious people who have been thus beset, and who make their fears the subject of earnest prayer, asking that this particular terror may be spared them, that this cup may be withdrawn from their shuddering lips. I do not believe that this is the right way of meeting the situation. One may pray as whole-heartedly as one will against the tendency to fear; but it is a great help to realise that the very experiences which seem now so overwhelming had little or no effect upon one in youthful and high-hearted days. It is not really that the quality of events alter; it is merely that one is losing vitality, and parting with the irresponsible hopefulness that did not allow one to brood, simply because there were so many other interesting and delightful things going on.

One must attack the disease, for it is a

disease, at the root; and it is of little use to shrink timidly from the particular evil, because when it is gone, another will take its place. We may pray for courage, but we must practise it; and the best way of meeting particular fears is to cultivate interests, distractions, amusements, which may serve to dispel them. We cannot begin to do that while we are under the dominion of a particular fear, for the strength of fear lies in its dominating and nauseating quality, so that it gives us a dreary disrelish for life; but if we really wish to combat it, we must beware of inactivity; it may be comfortable, as life goes on, to cultivate a habit of mild contemplation, but it is this very habit of mind which predisposes us to anxiety when anxiety comes. Dr. Johnson pointed out how comparatively rare it was for people who had manual labour to perform, and whose work lay in the open air, to suffer from hypochondriacal terrors. The truth is that we are made for labour, and we have by no means got rid of the necessity for it. We have to pay a price for the comforts of civilisation, and above all for the pleasures of inactivity. It is astonishing how quickly a definite task which one has to perform, whether one likes it or not, draws off a cloud of anxiety from one's spirit. I am myself liable to attacks of depression, not causeless depression, but a despondent exaggeration of small troubles. Yet in times of full work, when meetings have to be attended, papers tackled, engagements kept, I seldom find myself suffering from vague anxieties. It is simply astonishing that one cannot learn more common sense! I suppose that all people of anxious minds tend to find the waking hour a trying one. The mind, refreshed by sleep, turns sorrowfully to the task of surveying the difficulties which lie before it. And yet a hundred times have I discovered that life, which seemed at dawn nothing but a tangle of intolerable problems, has become at noon a very bearable and even interesting affair; and one should thus learn to appreciate the tonic value of occupation, and set oneself to discern some pursuit, if we have no compulsory duties, which may set the holy mill revolving, as Dante says; for it is the homely grumble of the gear which distracts us from the other sort of grumbling, the self-pitying frame of mind, which is the most fertile seed-plot of fear.

"How happy I was long ago; how little I guessed my happiness; how little I knew all that lay before me; how sadly and strangely afflicted I am!" These are the whispers of the evil demon of fearfulness; and they can only be checked by the murmur of wholesome and homely voices.

The old motto says, "Orare est laborare," "prayer is work"—and it is no less true that "laborare est orare," "work is prayer." The truth is that we cannot do without both; and when we have prayed for courage, and tried to rejoice in our beds, as the saints who are joyful in glory do, we had better spend no time in begging that money may be sent us to meet our particular need, or that health may return to us, or that this and that person may behave more kindly and considerately, but go our way to some perfectly commonplace bit of work, do it as thoroughly as we can, and simply turn our back upon the hobgoblin whose grimaces fill us with such uneasiness. He melts away in the blessed daylight over the volume or the account-book, in the simple talk about arrangements or affairs, and above all perhaps in trying to disentangle and relieve another's troubles and anxieties. We cannot get rid of fear by drugs or charms; we have to turn to the work which is the appointed solace of man, and which is the reward rather than the penalty of life.

XI

DR. JOHNSON

THERE is one great and notable instance in our annals which ought once and for all to dispose of the idea that there is anything weak or unmanly in finding fear a constant temptation, and that is the case of Dr. Johnson. Dr. Johnson holds his supreme station as the "figure" *par excellence* of English life for a number of reasons. His robustness, his wit, his reverence for established things, his secret piety are all contributory causes; but the chief of all causes is that the proportion in which these things were mixed is congenial to the British mind. The Englishman likes a man who is deeply serious without being in the least a prig; a man who is tender-hearted without being sentimental; he likes a rather combative nature, and enjoys repartee more than he enjoys humour. The Englishman values good sense above almost all qualities;

by a sensible man he means a man with a clear judgment of right and wrong, a man who is not taken in by pretences nor gulled by rhetoric; a man who can instinctively see what is important and what is unimportant. But of course the chief external reason, apart from the character of Johnson himself, for his supremacy of fame, is that his memory is enshrined in an incomparable biography. It shows the strange ineptness of Englishmen for literary and artistic criticism, their incapacity for judging a work of art on its own merits, their singular habit of allowing their disapprobation of a man's private character to depreciate his work, that an acknowledged critic like Macaulay could waste time in carefully considering whether Boswell was more fool or more knave, and triumphantly announce that he produced a good book by accident. Probably Boswell did not realise how matchless a biographer he was, though he was not disposed to belittle his own performances. But his unbridled interest in the smallest details, his power of hero-worship, his amazing style, his perception, his astonishing memory and the training he gave it, his superb dramatic faculty, which enabled him to arrange his other characters around the main figure, and to subordinate them all to his central emphasis—all these qualities are undeniable. Moreover he was himself the most perfect foil and contrast to Johnson that could be imagined, while he possessed in a unique degree the power of both stimulating and provoking his hero to animation and to wrath. Boswell may not have known what an artist he was, but he is probably one of the best literary artists who has ever lived.

But the supreme quality of his great book is this—that his interest in every trait of his hero, large and small, is so strong that he had none of that stiff propriety or chilly reserve which mars almost all English biographies. He did not care a straw whether this characteristic or that would redound to Johnson's credit. He saw that Johnson was a large-minded, large-hearted man, with an astonishing power of conversational expression, and an extremely picturesque figure as well. He perceived that he was big enough to be described in full, and that the shadows of his temperament only brought out the finer features into prominence.

Since the days of Johnson there are but two Englishmen whose lives we know in anything like the same detail—Ruskin and Carlyle. We know the life of Ruskin mainly from his own power of impassioned autobiography, and because he had the same sort of power of exhibiting both his charm and his weakness as Boswell had in dealing with Johnson. But Ruskin was not at all a typical Englishman; he had a very feminine side to his character, and though he was saved from sentimentality by his extreme trenchancy, and by his irritable temper, yet his whole temperament is beautiful, winning, attractive, rather than salient and picturesque. He had the qualities of a poet, a quixotic ideal, and an exuberant fancy; but though his spell over those who understand him is an almost magical one, his point of view is bound to be misunderstood by the ordinary man.

Carlyle's case is a different one again. There the evidence is mainly documentary. We know more about the Carlyle interior than we know of the history of any married pair since the world began. There is little doubt that if Carlyle could have had a Boswell, a biographer who could have rendered the effect of his splendid power of conversation, we might have had a book which could have been put on the same level as the life of Johnson, because Carlyle again was pre-eminently a "figure," a man made by nature to hold the enraptured attention of a circle. But it would have been a much more difficult task to represent Carlyle's talk than it was to represent Johnson's, because Carlyle was an inspired soliloquist, and supplied both objection and repartee out of his own mind. I think it probable that Carlyle was a typical Scotchman; he was more impassioned in his seriousness than Johnson, but he had a grimness which Johnson did not possess, and he had not Johnson's good-natured tolerance for foolish and well-meaning people. Carlyle himself had a good deal of Boswell's own gift, a power of minute and faithful observation, and a memory which treasured and reproduced characteristic details. If Carlyle had ever had the time or the taste to admire any human being as Boswell admired Johnson, he might have produced fully as great a book; but Carlyle had a prophetic impulse, an instinct for inverting tubs and preaching from them, a desire for telling the whole human race what to do and how to do it, which Johnson was too modest to claim.

There is but one other instance that I know in English literature of a man who had the Boswellian gift to the full, but who never had complete scope, and that was Hogg. If Hogg could have spent more of his life with Shelley, and had been allowed to complete his book, we might, I believe, have had a monument of the same kind.

But in the case of Boswell and Johnson, it is Boswell's magnificent scorn of reticence which has done the trick, like the spurt of acid, of which Browning speaks in one of his best similes. The final stroke of genius which has established the *Life of Johnson* so securely in the hearts of English readers, lies in the fact that Boswell has given us something to compassionate. As a rule the biographer cannot bear to evoke the smallest pity for his hero. The absence of female relatives in the case of Johnson was probably a part of his good fortune. No biographer likes, and seldom dares, to torture the sensibilities of a great man's widow and daughters. And the strength as well as the weakness of the feminine point of view is that women have a power not so much of not observing, as of actually obliterating the weaknesses of those whom they love. It is sentiment which ruins biographies, the sentiment that cannot bear the truth.

Boswell did not shrink from admitting the reader to a sight of Johnson's hypochondria, his melancholy fears, his dreary miseries, his dread of illness, his terror of death. Johnson's horror of annihilation was insupportable. He so revelled in life, in the contact and company of other human beings, that he once said that the idea of an infinity of torment was preferable to the thought of annihilation. He wrote, in his last illness, to his old friend Dr. Taylor:

"Oh! my friend, the approach of death is very dreadful. I am afraid to think on that which I know I cannot avoid. It is vain to look round and round for that help which cannot be had. Yet we hope and hope, and fancy that he who has lived to-day may live to-morrow. But let us learn to derive our hope only from God.

"In the meantime, let us be kind to one another. I have no friend now living but you and Mr. Hector that was the friend of my youth.—Do not neglect, sir, yours affectionately, SAM. JOHNSON."

Was ever the last fear put into such simple and poignant words as in the above letter? It is like that other saying of Johnson's, when all sorts of good reasons had been given why men should wish to be released from their troubles by death, "After all, it is a sad thing for a man to lie down and die." There is no more that can be said, and not the best reasons in the world for desiring to depart and have done with life can ever do away with that sadness.

Dr. Johnson supplies the clearest proof, if proof were needed, that no robustness of temperament, no genius of common sense, no array of rationality, no degree of courage, can save a man from the assaults of fear, and even of fear which the sufferer knows to be unreal. Some of the most severe and angry things which Johnson ever said were said to Boswell and others who persisted in discussing the question of death. Yet Johnson had no rational doubt of immortality, and believed with an almost childlike simplicity in the Christian faith. He was not afraid of pain, or of the act of dying; it was of the unknown conditions beyond the grave that he was afraid. Probably as a rule very robust people are so much occupied in living that they have little time to think of the future, while men and women who hold to life by a frail tenure are not much concerned at quitting a scene which is phantasmal and full of pain. But in Johnson we have the two extremes brought together. He was the most gregarious of men; he loved company so well that he would follow his friends to the very threshold, in the hope, as he once told Boswell, that they might perhaps return. When he was alone and undistracted, his melancholy came back upon him like a cloud. He tortured himself over the unprofitableness of his life, over his failure to achieve official prominence. He does not seem to have brooded over the favourite subject for Englishmen to lose heart over, namely, his financial position. It is a very significant fact in our English life that if at an inquest upon a suicide it can be established that a man has financial difficulties, a verdict of temporary insanity is instantly conceded. Loss of property rather than loss of affection is the thing which the Englishman thinks is likely to derange a man. But Johnson seems never to have been afraid of poverty, nor to have ever troubled about fame. He was very angry once when it was laughingly suggested to him that if he had gone to the Bar he might have been Lord Chancellor; and I have no doubt, as I have said, that one of his uncomfortable reflections was that he did not seem to himself to be in a position of influence and authority. But, apart from that, it is obvious that Johnson's broodings took the form of lamenting his own sinfulness and moral worthlessness: what the faults which troubled him were, it is hard to say. He does not seem to have been repentant about the mortification he caused others by his witty bludgeoning—indeed he considered himself a polite man! But I believe, from many slight indications, that Johnson was distressed by the consciousness of sensual impulses, though he held them in severe restraint. His habit of ejaculatory prayer was, I think, directed against this tendency. The agitation with which he once said that corruption had entered into his heart by means of a dream seems to me a proof of this. He took a tolerant view of the lapses of others, and of course the standard of the age was lax in this respect. But I have little doubt myself that here Johnson found himself often confronted with a sensuous tendency which he thought degrading, and which he constantly combated.

Apart from this, he was not afraid of illness in itself, except as a prelude of mortality. Indeed I believe that he took a hypochondriac pleasure in observing his symptoms minutely, and in dosing himself in all sorts of ways. His mysterious preoccupations with dried orange-peel had no doubt a medicinal end in view. But when it came to suffering pain and even to enduring operations, he had no tremors. His one constant fear was the fear of death. He kept it at arm's length, he loved any social amusement that banished it, but it is obvious, in several of his talks, when the subject was under discussion, that the cloud descended upon him suddenly and made him miserable. It was all summed up in this, that life was to his taste, that even when oppressed with gloom and depression, he never desired to escape. I have heard a great doctor say that he believed that human beings were very sharply divided in this respect, that there were some people in whom any extremity of prolonged anguish, bodily or mental, never produced the smallest desire to quit life; while there were others whose attachment to life was slight, and that a very little pressure of care or calamity developed a suicidal impulse. This is, I suppose, a question of vitality, not necessarily of activity of mind and body, but a deep instinctive desire to live; the thought of deliberate suicide was wholly unintelligible to Johnson, death was his ultimate fear, and however much he suffered from disease or depression, his intention to live was always inalienable.

His fear then was one which no devoutness of faith, no resolute tenacity of hope, no array of reasons could ever touch. It was simply the unknown that he feared. Life had not been an easy business for Johnson; he had known all the calamities of life, and he was familiar with the worst calamity of all, the causeless melancholy which makes life weary and distasteful without ever removing the certainty that it is in itself desirable.

We may see from all this that to attempt to seek a cure for fear in reason is foredoomed to failure, because fear lies in a region that is behind all reason. It exists in the depth of the spirit, as in the fallen gloom of the glimmering sea-deeps, and it can be touched by no activity of life and joy and sunlight on the surface, where the speeding sail moves past wind-swept headlands. We must follow it into those depths if we are to deal with it at all, and it must be vanquished in the region where it is born, and where it skulks unseen.

XII

TENNYSON, RUSKIN, CARLYLE

THERE were three great men of the nineteenth century of whom we know more than we know of most men, Carlyle, Ruskin, and Tennyson, in whose lives fear was a prominent element.

Tennyson has suffered no loss of fame, but he has suffered of late a certain loss of influence, which was bound to come, if simply from the tremendous domination which his writings exercised in his lifetime. He was undoubtedly one of the first word-artists who ever lived and wrote, but he was a great deal more than that; he was a great mystic, a man whose mind moved in a shining cloud of inspiration. He had the constitution and the temperament of a big Lincolnshire yeoman, with that simple rusticity that is said to have characterised Vergil. But his spirit dwelt apart, revolving dim and profound thoughts, brooding over mysteries; if he is lightly said to be Early Victorian, it is not because he was typical of his age, but because he contributed so much to make it what it was. While Browning lived an eager personal life, full of observation, zest, and passion, Tennyson abode in more impersonal thoughts. In the dawn of science, when there was a danger of life becoming over-materialised, contented with the first steps of swiftly apprehended knowledge, and with solutions which were no solutions at all, but only the perception of laws, Tennyson was the man of all others who saw that science had a deeply poetical side, and could enforce rather than destroy the religious spirit; he saw that a knowledge of processes was not the same thing as an explanation of impulses, and that while it was a little more clear in the light of science what was actually happening in the world, men were no nearer the perception of why it happened so, or why it happened at all. Tennyson saw clearly the wonders of astronomy and geology, and discerned that the laws of nature were nothing more than the habits, so to speak, of a power that was incredibly dim and vast, a power which held within itself the secrets of motion and rest, of death and life. Thus he claimed for his disciples not only the average thoughtful men, but the very best and finest minds of his generation who wished to link the past and the present together, and not to break with the old sanctities.

Tennyson's art suffered from the consciousness of his enormous responsibility, and where he failed was from his dread of unpopularity, or his fear of alienating the ordinary man. Browning was interested in ethical problems; his robust and fortunate temperament allowed him to bridge over with a sort of buoyant healthiness the gaps of his philosophy. But Tennyson's ethical failure lay in his desire to improve the occasion, and to rule out all impulses that had not a social and civic value. In the later "Idylls" he did his best to represent the prig trailing clouds of glory, and to discourage lawlessness in every form; but he was more familiar with the darker and grosser sides of life than he allowed to appear in his verse, which suffers from an almost prudish delicacy, which is more akin to respectability than to moral courage.

But all this was the shadow of a very sensitive and melancholy temperament. Comparatively little is known of the first forty years of his life; it is after that time that the elaborate legend begins. Till the time of his marriage, he must have been a constant anxiety to his friends; his gloom, his inertia, his drifting mooning ways, his hypochondria, his incapacity for any settled plan of life, all seemed to portend an ultimate failure. But this troubled inertness was the soil of his inspiration; his conceptions took slow and stately shape. He never suffered from the haste, which as Dante says "mars all decency of act." After that time he enjoyed a great domestic happiness, and practised considerable sociability. His terrifying demeanour, his amazing personal dignity and majesty, the certainty that he would say whatever came into his head, whether it was profound and solemn, or testy and discourteous, gave him a personal ascendancy that never disappointed a pilgrim.

But he lived all his life in a perpetual

melancholy, feeling the smallest slights acutely, hating at once obscurity and publicity, aware of his renown, yet shrinking from the evidences of it. He could be distracted by company, soothed by wine and tobacco; but left to itself, his mind fell helplessly down the dark slope into a sadness and a dreariness which deprived life of its savour. It was not that his dread was a definite one; he was strong and tough physically, and he regarded death with a solemn curiosity; but he had a sense of the profitlessness of vacant hours, unthrilled by beauty and delight, and had also a morbid pride, of the nature of vanity, which caused him to resent the smallest criticism of his works from the humblest reader. There are many stories of this, how he declaimed against the lust of gossip, which he called with rough appositeness "ripping up a man like a pig," and thanked God with all his heart and soul that he knew nothing of Shakespeare's private life; and in the same breath went on to say that he thought that his own fame was suffering from a sort of congestion, because he had received no letters about his poems for several days.

In later life he became very pessimistic, and believed that the world was sinking fast into dull materialism, petty selfishness, and moral anarchy. He had less opportunity of knowing what was going on in the world than most people, in his sheltered and secluded life, with his court of friends and worshippers. And indeed it was not a rational pessimism; it was but the shadow of his fear. And the fact remains that in spite of a life of great good fortune, and an undimmed supremacy of fame, he spent much of his time in fighting shadows, involved in clouds of darkness and dissatisfaction. That was no doubt the price he paid for his exquisite perception of beauty and his power of melodious expression. But we make a great mistake if we merely think of Tennyson as a rich and ample nature moving serenely through life. He was "black-blooded," he once said, adding, "like all the Tennysons." Doubtless he had in his mind his father, a man often deeply in the grip of melancholy. And the absurd legend, invented probably by Rossetti, contains a truth in it and may be quoted here. Rossetti said that he once went to dine with a friend in London, and was shown into a dimly lit drawing-room with no one to receive him. He went towards the fireplace, and suddenly to his surprise discovered an immensely tall man in evening dress lying prostrate on the hearthrug, his face downwards, in an attitude of prone despair. While he gazed, the stranger rose to his feet, looked fixedly at him, and said, "I must introduce myself; I am Octavius, the most morbid of the Tennysons."

With Ruskin we have a different case. He was brought up in the most secluded fashion, and though he was sharply enough disciplined into decorous behaviour by his very grim and positive mother, he was guarded like a precious jewel, and as he grew up he was endlessly petted and indulged. The Ruskins lived a very comfortable life in a big villa with ample grounds at Denmark Hill. Whatever the wonderful boy did was applauded and even dangerously encouraged, both in the way of drawing and of writing. Though he seems to have been often publicly snubbed by both his parents, it was more a family custom than anything else, and was accompanied by undisguised admiration and patent pride. They were his stupefied critics, when he read aloud his works in the family circle, and his father obediently produced large sums of money to gratify his brilliant son's artistic desire for the possession of Turner's paintings. Ruskin in his morbid moments, in later life, turned fiercely and unjustly against his fond and tender father. He accused him with an intemperate bitterness of having lavished everything upon him except the intelligent sympathy of which he stood in need, and his father's gentle and mournful apologies have an extraordinary beauty of puzzled and patient dignity about them.

When Ruskin went to Oxford, his mother went to reside there too, to look after her darling. One might have supposed that this would have involved Ruskin in ridicule, but he was petted and indulged by his fellow-undergraduates, who found his charm, his swift wit, his childlike waywardness, his freakish humour irresistible. Then he had a serious illness, and his first taste of misery;

he was afraid of death, he hated the constraints of invalid life and the grim interruption to his boundless energies and plans. Then came his first great book, and he strode full-fledged into fame. His amazing attractiveness, his talk, which combined incisiveness and fancy and humour and fire and gentleness, made him a marked figure from the first. Moreover, he had the command of great wealth, yet no temptation to be idle. The tale of Ruskin's industry for the next fifty years is one that would be incredible if it were not true. His brief and dim experience of married life seems hardly to have affected him. As a critic of art and ethics, as the writer of facile magnificent sentences, full of beauty and rhythm, as the composer of word-structures, apparently logical in form but deeply prejudiced and inconsequent in thought, he became one of the great influences of the day, and wielded not only power but real domination. The widespread delusion of the English educated classes, that they are interested in art, was of Ruskin's making. Then something very serious happened to him; a baffled passion of extraordinary intensity, a perception of the realities of life, the consciousness that his public indulged and humoured him as his parents had done, and admired his artistic advice without paying the smallest heed to his ethical principles—all these experiences broke over him, wearied as he was with excessive strain, like a bitter wave. But his pessimism took the noble form of an intense concern with the blindness and impenetrability of the world at large. He made a theory of political economy, which, peremptory and prejudiced as it is, is yet built on large lines, and has been fruitful in suggestiveness. But he tasted discouragement and failure in deep draughts. His parents frankly expressed their bewildered disappointment, his public looked upon him as a perverse man who was throwing away a beautiful message for the sake of a crabbed whim; and he fell into a fierce depression, alternating between savage energy and listless despondency, which lasted for several years, till at last the overwrought brain and mind gave way; and for the rest of his life he was liable to recurrent attacks of insanity, which cleared off and left him normal again, or as normal as he ever had been. Wide and eager as Ruskin's tenderness was, one feels that his heart was never really engaged; he was always far away, in a solitude full of fear, out of the reach of affection, always solemnly and mournfully alone. Ruskin was never really allied with any other human soul; he knew most of the great men of the day; he baited Rossetti, he petted Carlyle; he had correspondents like Norton, to whom he poured out his overburdened heart; but he was always the spoiled and indulged child of his boyhood, infinitely winning, provoking, wilful. He could not be helped, because he could never get away from himself; he could admire almost frenziedly, but he could not worship; he could not keep himself from criticism even when he adored, and he had a bitter superiority of spirit, a terrible perception of the imperfections and faults of others, a real despair of humanity.

I do not know exactly what the terrors which Ruskin suffered were—very few people will tell the tale of the valley of hobgoblins, or probably cannot! In the *Pilgrim's Progress* itself, the unreality of the spirits of fear, their secrecy and leniency, is very firmly and wittily told. They scream in their dens, sitting together, I have thought, like fowls in a roost. They come padding after the pilgrim, they show themselves obscurely, swollen by the mist at the corners of the road. They give the sense of being banded together in a numerous ambush, they can deceive eye and ear, and even nose with noisome stenches; but they cannot show themselves, and they cannot hurt. If they could be seen, they would be nothing but limp ungainly things that would rouse disdain and laughter and even pity, at anything at once so weak and so malevolent. But they are not like the demons of sin that can hamper and wound; they are just little gnomes and elves that can make a noise, and their strength is a spiteful and a puny thing.

Ruskin had no sordid or material fears; he had no fear of poverty, for he flung his father's hard-earned wealth profusely away; nor did he fear illness; indeed one of the bravest and most gallant things about him was the way in which he talked and wrote about his insane fits, described his haunted visions, told, half-ruefully, half-humorously, how he fought and struggled with his nurses, and made fun of the matter. That was a very courageous thing to do, because most people are ashamed of insanity, no doubt from the old sad ignorant tradition that it was the work of demoniacal agencies, and not a mere disease like other diseases. Half the tragedy of insanity is that it shocks people, and cannot be alluded to or spoken about; but one can take the sting out of almost any calamity if one can make fun of it, and this Ruskin did.

But he was wounded by his fears, as we most of us are, not only through his vanity but through his finest emotions. He felt his impotence and his failure. He had thought of his gift of language as one might think of a magic wand which one can wave, and thus compel duller spirits to do one's bidding. Ruskin began by thinking that there was not much amiss with the world except a sort of pathetic stupidity; and he thought that if only people could be told, clearly and loudly enough, what was right, they would do it gladly; and then it dawned upon him by slow degrees that the confusion was far deeper than that, that men mostly did not live in motives but in appetites. And so he fell into a sort of noble rage with the imperfection of mortal things; and one of the clearest signs, as he himself knew, that he was drifting into one of the mind-storms which swept across him, was that in these moods everything that people said or wrote had power to arouse his irritation, to interrupt his work, to break his sleep, and to show him that he was powerless indeed. What he feared was derision, and the good-natured indifferent stolidity that is worse than any derision, and the knowledge that, with all his powers and perceptions, his common-sense, which was great, and his sense of responsibility, he was treated by the world like a spoilt child, charming even in his wrath, who had full license to be as vehement as he liked, with the understanding that no one would act on his advice.

I often go to Brantwood, which is a sacred place indeed, and see with deep emotion the little rooms, with all their beautiful treasures, and all the great accumulations of that fierce industry of mind, and remember that in that peaceful background a man of exquisite genius fought with sinister shadows, and was worsted in the fight, for a time; because the last ten years of that long life were a time of serene waiting for death, a beguiling by little childish and homely occupations the heavy hours: he could uplift his voice no more, often could hardly frame an intelligible thought. But meanwhile his great message went on rippling out to the world, touching heart after heart into light and hope, and doing, insensibly and graciously, by the spirit, the very thing he had failed to do by might and power.

And then we come to Carlyle, and here we are on somewhat different ground. Carlyle had a colossal quarrel with the age, but he thought very little of the message of beauty and peace. His idea of the world was that of a stern combative place, with the one hope a strenuous and grim righteousness; Carlyle thought of the world as a place where cheats and liars cozened and beguiled men, for their own advantage, with all sorts of shams and pretences: but he did not really know the world; he put down to individual action and deliberate policy much that was due simply to the prevalence of tradition and system, and to the complexity of civilisation. He was so fierce an individualist himself that he credited everyone else with purpose and prejudice. He did not realise the vast preponderance of helpless good-nature and muddled kindliness. The mistake of much of Carlyle's work is that it is too poignantly dramatic, and bristles with intention and significance; and he did not allow sufficiently for the crowd of vague supers who throng the background of the stage. Neither did he ever go about the world with his eyes open for general facts. Wherever he was, he was intensely observant, but he spent his days either in a fierce absorption of work, blind even to the sorrow and discomfort of his wife, or taking rapid tours to store his mind with the details of historical scenes, or in the big houses of wealthy people, where he kept much to himself, stored up irresistibly absurd caricatures of the other guests, and lamented his own inaction. I have never been able to discover exactly why Carlyle spent so much time in staying at great houses, deriding and satirising everything he set eyes upon; it was, I believe, vaguely gratifying to him to have raised himself unaided into the highest social stratum; and the old man was after all a tremendous aristocrat at heart. Or else he skulked with infinite melancholy in his mother's house, being waited upon and humoured, and indulging his deep and true family affection. But he was a solitary man for the most part, and mixed with men, involved in a cloud of his own irresistibly fantastic and whimsical talk; for his real gift was half-humorous, half-melancholy improvisation rather than deliberate writing.

But it is difficult to discern in all this what his endless and plangent melancholy was concerned with. He had a very singular physical frame, immensely tough and wiry, with an imagination which emphasized and particularised every slight touch of bodily disorder. When he was at work, he toiled like a demon day after day, entirely and vehemently absorbed. When he was not at work he suffered from dreary reaction. He fought out in early days a severe moral combat, and found his way to a belief in God which was very different from his former Calvinism. Carlyle can by no stretch of the word be called a Christian, but he was one of the most thorough-going Deists that ever lived. The terror that beset him in that first great conflict was a ghastly fear of his own insignificance, and a horrible suspicion that the world was made on fortuitous and indifferent lines. His dread was that of being worsted, in spite of all his eager sensibility and immense desire to do a noble work, of being crushed, silenced, thrown ruthlessly on the dust-heap of the world. He learned a fiery sort of Determinism, and a faith in the stubborn power of the will, not to achieve anything, but to achieve something.

Yet after this tremendous conflict, described in *Sartor Resartus*, where he found himself at bay with his back to the wall, he never had any ultimate doubt again of his own purpose. Still, it brought him no serenity; and I suppose there is no writer in the world whose letters and diaries are so full of cries of anguish and hopelessness. He was crushed under the sense of the world's immensity; his own observation was so microscopic, his desire to perceive and know so strong, his appetite for definiteness so profound, that I feel that Carlyle's terror was like that of a mite in an enormous cheese, longing to explore it all, lost in the high-flavoured dusk, and conscious of a scale of mystery so vast that it humiliated a brain that wanted to know the truth about everything. In these sad hours—and they were numerous and protracted—he felt like a knight worn out by conflict, under a listless enchantment which he could not break. I know few confessions that are so filled with gleams of high poetry and beauty as many of these solitary lamentations. But I believe that the terrors that Carlyle had to face were the terrors of a swift, clear-sighted, feverishly active, intuitive brain, prevented by mortal weakness and frailty from dealing as he desired with the dazzling immensity and intricacy of the world's life and history.

I feel no real doubt of this, because Carlyle's passion for accurate and minute knowledge, his intense interest in temperament and character, his almost unequalled power of observation —which is really the surest sign of genius— come out so clearly all through his life, that his finite limitations must have been of the nature of a torture to him. One who desired to know the truth about everything so vehemently, was crushed and bewildered by the narrow range and limited scope of his own insatiable thought. His power of expressing all that he saw and felt, so delicately, so humorously, and at times so tenderly, must have beguiled his sadness more than he knew. It was Ruskin who said that he could never fit the two sides of the puzzle together— on the one side the awful dejection and despondency which Carlyle always claimed to feel in the presence of his work, as a dredger in lakes of mud and as a sorter of mountains of rubbish, and on the other side the endless relish for salient traits, and the delighted apprehension of quality which emerges so clearly in all he wrote.

But it is clear that Carlyle suffered ceaselessly, though never unutterably. He was a matchless artist, with an unequalled gift of putting into vivid words everything he experienced; but his sadness was a disease of the imagination, a fear, not of anything definite—for he never even saw the anxieties that were nearest to him—but a nightmare dream of chaos and whirling forces all about him, a dread of slipping off his own very fairly comfortable perch into oceans of confusion and dismay.

XIII

CHARLOTTE BRONTË

I DOUBT if the records of intimate biography contain a finer object-lesson against fear and all its obsessions than the life of Charlotte Brontë. She was of a temperament which in many ways was more open to the assaults of fear than any which could well be devised. She was frail and delicate, liable to acute nervous depression, intensely shy and sensitive, and susceptible as well; that is to say that her shyness did not isolate her from her kind; she wanted to be loved, respected, even admired. When she did love, she loved with fire and passion and desperate loyalty.

Her life was from beginning to end full of sharp and tragic experiences. She was born and brought up in a bleak moorland village, climbing steeply and grimly to the edge of heathery uplands. The bare parsonage, with its little dark rooms, looks out on a churchyard paved with graves. Her father was a kindly man, but essentially moody and solitary. He took all his meals alone, walked alone, sate alone. Her mother died of cancer, when she was but a child. Then she was sent to an ill-managed austere school, and here when she was nine years old her two elder sisters died. She took service two or three times as a governess, and endured agonies of misunderstanding, suspicious of her employers, afraid of her pupils, longing for home with an intense yearning. Then she went out to a school at Brussels, where under the teaching of M. Héger, a gifted professor, her mind and heart awoke, and she formed for him a strange affection, half an intellectual devotion, half an unconscious passion, which deprived her of her peace of mind. Her sad and wistful letters to him, lately published, were disregarded by him, partly because his wife was undoubtedly jealous of the relation, partly because he was disconcerted by the emotion he had aroused. Her brother, a brilliant, wayward, and in some ways attractive boy, got into disgrace, and drifted home, where he tried to console himself with drink and opium. After three years of this horrible life, he died, and within twelve months her two surviving sisters, Emily and Anne, developed consumption and died. As Robert Browning says, there indeed was "trouble enough for one!"

Now it must be borne in mind that her temperament was naturally hypochondriacal.

Let me quote a passage dealing with the same experience; it is undoubtedly autobiographical, though it comes from *Villette*, into which Charlotte Brontë threw the picture of her own solitary experiences in Brussels. She is left alone at the *pensionnat* in the vacation, strained by work and anxiety, and tortured by exhaustion, restlessness, and sleeplessness :—

"One day, perceiving this growing illusion, I said, 'I really believe my nerves are getting overstretched: my mind has suffered somewhat too much; a malady is growing upon it —what shall I do? How shall I keep well?'

"Indeed there was no way to keep well under the circumstances. At last a day and night of peculiarly agonising depression were succeeded by physical illness; I took perforce to my bed. About this time the Indian summer closed, and the equinoctial storms began; and for nine dark and wet days, of which the hours rushed on all turbulent, deaf, dishevelled—bewildered with sounding hurricane—I lay in a strange fever of the nerves and blood. Sleep went quite away. I used to rise in the night, look round for her, beseech her earnestly to return. A rattle of the window, a cry of the blast only replied—Sleep never came!

"I err. She came once, but in anger. Impatient of my importunity she brought with her an avenging dream. By the clock of St. Jean Baptiste, that dream remained scarce fifteen minutes—a brief space, but sufficing to wring my whole frame with unknown anguish; to confer a nameless experience that had the hue, the mien, the terror, the very tone of a visitation from eternity. Between twelve and one that night a cup was forced to my lips, black, strong, strange, drawn from no well, but filled up seething from a bottomless and boundless sea. Suffering, brewed in temporal or calculable measure, and mixed for mortal lips, tastes not as this suffering tasted. Having drank and woke, I thought all was over: the end come and passed by. Trembling fearfully—as consciousness returned—ready to cry out on some fellow-creature to help me, only that I knew no fellow-creature was near enough to catch the wild summons—Goton in her far distant attic could not hear—I rose on my knees in bed. Some fearful hours went over me; indescribably was I torn, racked and oppressed in mind. Amidst the horrors of that dream I think the worst lay here. Methought the well-loved dead, who had loved *me* well in life, met me elsewhere alienated; galled was my inmost spirit with an unutterable sense of despair about the future. Motive there was none why I should try to recover or wish to live; and yet quite unendurable was the pitiless and haughty voice in which Death challenged me to engage his unknown terrors. When I tried to pray I could only utter these words:—

"'From my youth up Thy terrors have I suffered with a troubled mind.'"

The deep interest of this experience is that it was endured by one who was not only intellectually endowed beyond most women of her time, but whose sanity, reasonableness, and moral force were conspicuously strong. Charlotte Brontë was not one of those impulsive and imaginative women who are the prey of every fancy. Throughout the whole of her career, she was for ever compelling her frail and sensitive temperament, with indomitable purpose, to perform whatever she had undertaken to do. There never was anyone who lived so sternly by principle and reason, or who so maintained her self-control in the face of sorrow, disaster, unhappiness, and bereavement. She never gave way to feeble or morbid self-accusation, and therefore the fact that she could thus have suffered is a sign that this unnamed terror can coexist with a dauntless courage and an essential self-command.

Here again is the cry of a desolate heart! She had been going through her sisters' papers not long after their death, and wrote to her great friend: "I am both angry and surprised at myself for not being in better spirits; for not growing accustomed, or at least resigned, to the solitude and isolation of my lot. But my late occupation left a result, for some days and indeed still, very painful. The reading over of papers, the renewal of remembrances, brought back the pangs of bereavement and occasioned a depression of spirits well-nigh intolerable. For one or two nights I hardly knew how to get on till morning; and when morning came I was still haunted by a sense of sickening distress. I tell you these things because it is absolutely necessary to me to have *some* relief. You will forgive me and not trouble yourself, or imagine that I am one whit worse than I say. It is quite a mental ailment, and I believe and hope is better now. I think so, because I can speak about it, which I never can when grief is at its worst. I thought to find occupation and interest in writing when alone at home, but hitherto my efforts have been in vain: the deficiency of every stimulus is so complete. You will recommend me, I dare say, to go from home; but that does no good, even could I again leave papa with an easy mind. . . . I cannot describe what a time of it I had after my return from London and Scotland. There was a reaction that sank me to the earth, the deadly silence, solitude, depression, desolation were awful; the craving for companionship, the hopelessness of relief were what I should dread to feel again." Or again, in a somewhat calmer mood, she writes: "I feel to my deep sorrow, to my humiliation, that it is not in my power to bear the canker of constant solitude. I had calculated that when shut out from every enjoyment, from every stimulus but what could be desired from intellectual exertion, my mind would rouse itself perforce. It is not so. Even intellect, even imagination will not dispense with the ray of domestic cheerfulness, with the gentle spur of family discussions. Late in the evening and all through the nights, I fall into a condition of mind which turns entirely to the past—to memory, and memory is both sad and relentless. This will never do, and will produce no good. I tell you this that you may check false anticipations. You cannot help me, and must not trouble yourself in any shape to sympathise with me. It is my cup, and I must drink it as others do theirs."

It would be difficult to create a picture of

more poignant suffering; yet she was at this time a famous writer. She had published *Jane Eyre* and *Shirley*, and on her visits to London, to her hospitable publisher, had found herself welcomed, honoured, fêted. The great lions of the literary world had flocked eagerly to meet her. Even these simple festivities were accompanied by a deadly sense of strain, anxiety, and exhaustion. Mrs. Gaskell describes how a little later she met Charlotte Brontë at a quiet country-house, and how Charlotte was reduced from tolerable health to a bad nervous headache by the announcement that they were going to drive over in the afternoon to have tea at a neighbour's house—the prospect of meeting strangers was so alarming to her.

But in spite of this agonising susceptibility and vulnerability, there is never the least touch either of sentimentality or self-pity about Charlotte Brontë. She stuck to her duty and faced life with an infinity of patient courage. One of her friends said of her that no one she had ever known had sacrificed more to others, or done it with a fuller consciousness of what she was sacrificing. If duty and affection bade her act, no sense of weakness or of inclination had any power over her. She was afraid of life, but she stood up to it; she was never crushed or broken. Consider the circumstances under which she began to write *Jane Eyre*. She had written her novel *The Professor*, and it was returned to her nine several times, by publisher after publisher. Her father was threatened with blindness. She had taken him to Manchester for an operation, installed him in lodgings, and settled down alone to nurse him. The ill-fated *Professor* came back to her once more with a polite refusal. That very day she wrote the first lines of *Jane Eyre*. Later on too, with her brother dying of opium and drink, she had begun *Shirley*, and she finished it after the deaths of her sisters. She was perfectly merciless to herself, saw no reason why she should be spared any sorrow or suffering or ill-health, but looked upon it all as a stern but not unjust discipline. She had one of the most passionately affectionate natures both in friendship and home relations—"my hot tenacious heart," she once says! But there was no touch of softness or sentimentality about her; she never feebly condoned weaknesses; her observation of people was minute, her judgment of them severe and even satirical. Her letters abound in pungent humour and acute perception; and her idea of charity was not that of mild and muddled tolerance. She had a vein of frank and rather bitter irony when she was indignant, and she could return stroke for stroke.

She knew well that, whatever life was meant to be, it was not intended to be an easy business; but she did not face it stoically or indifferently; she had a fierce desire for knowledge, culture, ideas; she was ambitious; and above everything she desired to be loved; yet she did not think of love in the way in which all English romancers had treated it for over a century, as a condescending hand held out by a superior being, for the glory of which a woman submitted to a more or less contented servitude; but as a glowing equality of passion and worship, in which two hearts clasped each other close, with a sacred concurrence of soul. And thus it was that she and Robert Browning, above all other writers of the century, put the love of man and woman in the true light, as the supreme worth of life; not as a half-sensuous excitement, with lapses and reactions, but as a great and holy mystery of devotion and service and mutual help. She too had her little taste of love. Mr. Nicholls, her father's curate, a man of deep tenderness behind his quiet homely ways, had proposed to her; she had refused him; but his suffering and bewilderment had touched her deeply, and at last she consented, though she went to her wedding in fear and dread; but she was rewarded, and for a few short months tasted a calm and sweet happiness, the joy of being needed and desired, and at the same time guarded and tended well. Her pathetic words, when she knew from his lips that she must die, "God will not part us—we have been so happy," are full of the deepest tragedy.

I say again that I know of no instance among the most intimate records of the human heart, in which life was faced with such splendid courage as it was by Charlotte Brontë. It contained so many things which she desired—art, beauty, thought, peace, deep and tender relations, and the supreme crown of love. But she never dreamed of trying to escape or shirk her lot. After her first great success with *Jane Eyre*, she might have lived life on her own lines; her writing meant wealth to one of her simple tastes; and as her closest friend said, if she had chosen to set up a house of her own, she would have been gratefully thanked for any kindness she might have shown to her household, instead of being, as she was, ruthlessly employed and even tyrannised over. Consider how a young authoress, with that splendid success to her credit, would nowadays be made much of and tended, begged to consult her own wishes and make her own arrangements. But Charlotte Brontë hated notoriety, and took her fame with a shrinking and modest amazement. She never gave herself airs, or displayed any affectation, or caught at any flattery. She just went back to her tragic home, and carried the burden of housekeeping on her frail shoulders. The simplicity, the delicacy, the humility of it all is above praise. If ever there was a human being who might have pleaded to be excused from any gallant battling with life because of her bleak, comfortless, unhappy surroundings, and her own sensitive temperament, it was Charlotte Brontë. But instead of that she fought silently with disaster and unhappiness, neither pitying herself for her destiny, nor taking the smallest credit for her tough resistance. It does not necessarily prove that all can wage so equal a fight with fears and sorrows; but it shows at least that an indomitable resolution can make a noble thing out of a life from which every circumstance of romance and dignity seems to be purposely withdrawn.

I do not think that there is in literature a more inspiring and heartening book than Mrs. Gaskell's *Life of Charlotte Brontë.* The book was written with a fine frankness and a daring indiscretion which cost Mrs. Gaskell very dear. It remains as one of the most matchless and splendid presentments of duty and passion and genius, waging a perfectly undaunted fight with life and temperament, and carrying off the spoils not only of undying fame, but the far more supreme crown of moral force. Charlotte Brontë never doubted that she had been set in the forefront of the battle, and that her first concern was with the issues of life and sorrow and death. She died at thirty-eight, at a time when many men and women have hardly got a firm hold of life at all, or have parted with weak illusions. Yet years before she had said sternly to a friend who was meditating a flight from hard conditions of life: "The right course is that which necessitates the greatest sacrifice of self-interest." Many people could have said that, but I know no figure who more relentlessly and loyally carried out the principle than Charlotte Brontë, or who waged a more vigorous and tenacious battle with every onset of fear. "My conscience tells me," she once wrote about an anxious decision, "that it would be the act of a moral poltroon to let the fear of suffering stand in the way of improvement. But suffer I shall. No matter!"

XIV

JOHN STERLING

I BELIEVE that the most affecting, beautiful, and grave message ever written from a death-bed is John Sterling's last letter to Carlyle. It reflects, perhaps, something of Carlyle's own fine manner, but then Sterling had long been Carlyle's friend and confidant.

Before I give it, let me add a brief account of Sterling. He was some ten years Carlyle's junior, the son of the redoubtable Edward Sterling, the leader-writer of the *Times*, a man who in his day wielded a mighty influence. Carlyle describes the father's way of life, how he spent the day in going about London, rolling into clubs, volubly questioning and talking; then returned home in the evening, and condensed it all into a leader, "and is found," said Carlyle, "to have hit the essential purport of the world's immeasurable babblement that day with an accuracy above all other men."

The younger Sterling, Carlyle's friend, was at Cambridge for a time, but never took his degree; he became a journalist, wrote a novel, tales, plays, endless poems—all of thin and vapid quality. His brief life, for he died at thirty-eight, was a much disquieted one; he travelled about in search of health, for he was early threatened with consumption; for a short time he was a curate in the English Church, but drifted away from that. He lived for a time at Falmouth, and afterwards at Ventnor. He must have been a man of extraordinary charm, and with quite unequalled powers of conversation. Even Carlyle seems to have heard him gladly, and that is no ordinary compliment, considering Carlyle's own volubility, and the agonies, occasionally suppressed but generally trenchantly expressed, with which Carlyle listened to other well-known talkers like Coleridge and Macaulay.

Carlyle certainly had a very deep affection and admiration for Sterling; he rains down praises upon him, in that wonderful little biography, which is probably the finest piece of work that Carlyle ever did.

He speaks of Sterling as "brilliant, beautiful, cheerful with an ever-flowing wealth of ideas, fancies, imaginations . . . with frank affections, inexhaustible hopes, audacities, activities, and general radiant vivacity of heart and intelligence, which made the presence of him an illumination and inspiration wherever he went."

But all Carlyle's love and admiration for his friend did not induce him to praise Sterling's writings; he looked upon him as a poet, but without the gift of expression. He says that all Sterling's work was spoilt by over-haste, and "a lack of due inertia." The fact is that Sterling was a sort of *improvisatore*, and what was beautiful and natural enough when poured out in talk, and with the stimulus of congenial company, grew pale and indistinct when he wrote it down; he had, in fact, no instinct for art or for design, and he failed whenever he tried to mould ideas into form.

The shadow of illness darkened about him, and he spent long periods in prostrate seclusion, tended by his wife and children, unable to write or talk or receive his friends. Then a terrible calamity befell him. His mother, to whom he was devotedly attached, died after a long illness, Sterling not being allowed to go to her, or to leave his own sick-room. He received the news one morning by letter, that all was over, went in to tell his wife, who was ill; while they were talking, his wife became faint, and died two hours later. So that within a few hours he lost the two human beings whom he most devotedly loved, and on whom he most depended for sympathy and help.

But in all Sterling's sorrows and illnesses, he never seems to have lost his interest in life and thought, in ideas, questions, and problems. Again and again he came back to the surface, with an irrepressible zest and freshness, and even gaiety, until at last all hope of life was extinguished. He lay dying for many weeks, and it was then that he wrote his last letter to Carlyle, which must be given in full :—

HILLSIDE, VENTNOR,
10th August 1844.

MY DEAR CARLYLE,—For the first time for many months it seems possible to send you a few words; merely, however, for Remembrance and Farewell. On higher matters there is nothing to say. I tread the common road into the great darkness, without any thought of fear, and with very much of hope. Certainty indeed I have none. With regard to you and me I cannot begin to write; having nothing for it but to keep shut the lid of those secrets with all the iron weights that are in my power. Towards me it is still more true than towards England that no man has been and done like you. Heaven bless you! If I can lend a hand when THERE, that will not be wanting. It is all very strange, but not one hundredth part so sad as it seems to the standers-by.

Your Wife knows my mind towards her, and will believe it without asseverations.—Yours to the last, JOHN STERLING.

That letter may speak for itself. In its dignity, its nobleness, its fearlessness, it is one of the finest human documents I know. But let it be remembered that it is not the letter of a mournful and heart-broken man, turning his back on life in an ecstasy of despair; but the letter of one who had taken a boundless delight in life, had known upon equal terms most of the finest intellects of the day, and had been frankly recognised by them as a chosen spirit. All Sterling's designs for life and work had been slowly and surely thwarted by the pressure of hopeless illness; yet he had never complained or fretted or brooded, or indulged in any bitter recriminations against his destiny. That seems to me a very heroic attitude; while the letter itself, in its perfect frankness and courage, without a touch of solemnity or affectation, or any trace of craven shrinking from his doom, makes it in its noble simplicity one of the finest "last words" that I have ever read, and finer, I verily believe, than any flight of poetical imagination.

A few days later he sent Carlyle some stanzas of verse, "written," says Carlyle, "as if in star-fire and immortal tears; which are among my sacred possessions, to be kept for myself alone."

A few weeks before he wrote his last letter to Carlyle, Sterling had written a letter to his son, who was then a boy at school in London. In that he says: "When I fancy how you are walking in the same streets, and moving along the same river, that I used to watch so intently, as if in a dream, when younger than you are—I could gladly burst into tears, not of grief, but with a feeling that there is no name for. Everything is so wonderful, great and holy, so sad and yet not bitter, so full of Death and so bordering on Heaven. Can you understand anything of this? If you can, you will begin to know what a serious matter our Life is; how unworthy and stupid it is to trifle it away without heed; what a wretched, insignificant, worthless creature anyone comes to be, who does not as soon as possible bend his whole strength, as in stringing a stiff bow, to doing whatever task lies first before him."

That again is a noble letter; but over it I think there lies a little shadow of regret, a sense that he had himself wasted some of the force of life in vague trifling; but even that mood had passed away in the nearness of the great impending change, leaving him upborne upon the greatness of God, in deep wonder and hope, knowing nothing more, in his weariness and his suffering, but the calmness of the Eternal Will.

XV

INSTINCTIVE FEAR

THE fears then from which men suffer, and even the greatest men not least, seem to be strangely complicated by the fact that nature does not seem to work as fast in the physical world as in the mental world. The mosquitoes of South American swamps are all fitted with a perfect tool-box of implements for piercing the hides of warm-blooded animals and drawing blood, although warm-blooded animals have long ceased to exist in those localities. But as the mosquito is one of the few creatures which can propagate its kind without ever partaking of food, the mosquito has therefore not died out; and though for many generations billions upon billions of mosquitoes have never had a chance of doing what they seem born to do, they have not discarded their apparatus. If mosquitoes could reason and philosophise, the prospect of such a meal might remain as a far-off and inspiring ideal of life and conduct, a thing which heroes in the past had achieved, and which might be possible again if they remained true to their highest instincts. So it is with humanity. Many of our fears do not correspond to any real danger; they are part of a panoply which we inherit, and have to do with the instinct of self-preservation. We are exposed to dangers still, dangers of infection for instance, but we have developed no instinctive fear which helps us to recognise the presence of infection. We take rational precautions against it when we recognise it, but the vast prevalence and mortality of consumption a generation or two ago was due to the fact that men did not recognise consumption as infectious; and many fine lives—Keats and Emily Brontë, to name but two—were sacrificed to careless proximity as well as to devoted tendance; but here nature, with all her instinct of self-preservation, did not hang out any danger signal, or provide human beings with any instinctive fear to protect them. Our instinctive fears, such as our fear of darkness and solitude, and our suspicion of strangers, seem to date from a time when such conditions were really dangerous, though they are so no longer.

At the same time the development of the imaginative faculty has brought with it a whole series of new terrors, through our power of anticipating and picturing possible calamities; while our increased sensitiveness as well as our more sentimental morality expose us to yet another range of fears. Consider the dread which many of us feel at the prospect of a painful interview, our avoidance of an unpleasant scene, our terror of arousing anger. The basis of all this is the primeval dread of personal violence. We are afraid of arousing anger, not because we expect to be assailed by blows and wounds, but because our far-off ancestors expected anger to end in an actual assault. We may know that we shall emerge from an unpleasant interview unscathed in fortune and in limb, but we anticipate it with a quite irrational terror, because we are still haunted by fears which date from a time when injury was the natural outcome of wrath. It may be our duty, and we may recognise it to be our duty, to make a protest of an unpleasant kind, or to withstand the action of an irritable person; but though we know well enough that he has no power to injure us, the flashing eye, the distended nostril, the rising pallor, the uplifted voice have a disagreeable effect on our nerves, although we know well that no physical disaster will result from it. Mrs. Browning, for instance, though she had high moral courage and tenacity of purpose, could not face an interview with her father, because an exhibition of his anger caused her to faint away on the spot. One does not often experience this whiff of violent anger in middle life; but the other day I had occasion to speak to a colleague of mine on a Board of which I am a member, at the conclusion of a piece of business in which I had proposed and carried a certain policy. I did not know that he disapproved of the policy in question, but I found on speaking to him that he was in a towering passion at my having opposed the policy which he preferred. He grew pale with rage; the hair on his head seemed to bristle, his eyes flashed fire; he slammed down a bundle of papers in his hand on the table, he stamped with passion; and I confess that it was profoundly disturbing and disconcerting. I felt for a moment that sickening sense of misgiving with which as a little boy one confronted an angry schoolmaster. Though I knew that I had a perfect right to my opinion, though I recognised that my sensations were quite irrational, I felt myself confronted with something demoniacal and insane, and the basis of it was, I am sure, physical and not moral terror. If I had been bullied or chastised as a child, I should be able to refer the discomfort I felt to old associations. But I feel no doubt that my emotion was something far more primeval than that, and that the dumb and atrophied sense of self-preservation was at work. The fear then that I felt was an instinctive thing, and was experienced in the inner nature and not in the rational mind; and the perplexity of the situation arises from the fact that such fear cannot be combated by rational considerations. Though no harm whatever resulted or could result from such an interview, yet I am certain that the prospect of such an outbreak would make me in the future far more cautious in dealing with this particular man, more anxious to conciliate him, and probably more disposed to compromise a matter.

Such an incident makes one unpleasantly aware of the quality of one's nature and temperament. It shows one that though one may have a strong moral and intellectual sense of what is the right and sensible course to take, one may be sadly hampered in carrying it out, by this secret and hidden instinct of which one may be rationally ashamed, but which is characteristic of what seems to be the stronger and more vital part of one's self.

The whole of civilisation is a combat between these two forces, a struggle between the rational and the instinctive parts of the mind. The instinctive mind bids one follow profit, need, advantage, the pleasure of the moment; the rational part of the mind bids one abstain, resist, balance contingencies, act in accordance with a moral standard. Many such abstentions become a mere matter of habit. If one is hungry and thirsty, and meets a child carrying bread or milk, one has no impulse to seize the food and eat it. One does not reflect upon the possible outcome of following the impulse of plunder; it simply does not enter one's head so to act. And there is of course a slow process going on in the world by which this moral restraint is becoming habitual and instinctive; but notably in the case of fear our instinct is a belated one, and results in many causeless and baseless anxieties which our reason in vain assures us are wholly false.

What then is our practical way of escape from the dominion of these shadows? Not, I am sure, in any resolute attempt to combat them by rational weapons; the rational argument, the common-sense consolation, only touches the rational part of the mind; we have got to get behind and below that, we have got somehow to fight instinct by instinct, and quell the terror in its proper home. By our finite nature we are compelled to attend to one thing at a time, and thus if we use rational argument, we are recognising the presence of the irrational fear; it is of little use then to array our advantages against our disadvantages, our blessings against our sufferings, as Michael Finsbury did with such small effect in *The Wrong Box;* our only chance is to turn tail altogether, and try to set some other dominant instinct at work; while we remember, we shall continue to suffer; our best chance lies in forgetting, and we can only do that by calling some other dominant emotion into play.

And here comes in the peculiarly paralysing effect of these baser emotions. As Victor Hugo once said, in a fine apophthegm, "Despair yawns." Fear and anxiety bring with them a particular kind of physical fatigue which makes us listless and inert. They lie on the spirit with a leaden dullness, which takes from us all possibility of energy and motion. Who does not know the instinct, when one is crushed and tortured by depression, to escape into solitude and silence, and to let the waves and streams flow over one. That is a universal instinct, and it is not wholly to be disregarded; it shows that to torture oneself into rational activity is of little use, or worse than useless.

WHERE NO FEAR WAS

When I was myself a sufferer from long nervous depression, and had to face a social gathering, I used out of very shame, and partly I think out of a sense of courtesy due to others, to galvanise myself into a sort of horrid merriment. The dark tide flowed on beneath in its sore and aching channels. It was common enough then for some sympathetic friend to say, "You seemed better to-night—you were quite yourself; that is what you want; if you would only make the effort and go out more into society, you would soon forget your troubles." There is something in it, because the sick mind must be persuaded if possible not to grave its dolorous course too indelibly in the temperament; but no one else could see the acute and intolerable reaction which used to follow such a strain, or how, the excitement over, the suffering resumed its sway over the exhausted self with an insupportable agony. I am sure that in my long affliction I never suffered more than after occasions when I was betrayed by excitement into argument or lively talk, and the worst spasms of melancholy that I ever endured were the direct and immediate results of such efforts.

The counteracting force in fact must be an emotional and instinctive one, not a rational and deliberate one; and this must be our next endeavour, to see in what direction the counterpoise must lie.

In depression then, and when causeless fears assail us, we must try to put the mind in easier postures, to avoid excess and strain, to live more in company, to do something different. Human beings are happiest in monotony and settled ways of life; but these also develop their own poisons, like sameness of diet, however wholesome it may be. It is, I believe, an established fact that most people cannot eat a pigeon a day for fourteen days in succession; a pigeon is not unwholesome, but the digestion cannot stand iteration. There is an old and homely story of a man who went to a great doctor suffering from dyspepsia. The doctor asked him what he ate, and he said that he always lunched off bread and cheese. "Try a mutton chop," said the doctor. He did so with excellent results. A year later he was ill again and went to the same doctor, who put him through the same catechism. "What do you have for luncheon?" said the doctor. "A chop," said the patient, conscious of virtuous obedience. "Try bread and cheese," said the doctor. "Why," said the patient, "that was the very thing you told me to avoid." "Yes," said the doctor, "and I tell you to avoid a chop now. You are suffering not from diet, but from monotony of diet—and you want a change."

The principle holds good of ordinary life; it is humiliating to confess it, but these depressions and despondencies which beset us are often best met by very ordinary physical remedies. It is not uncommon for people who suffer from them to examine their consciences, rake up forgotten transgressions, and feel themselves to be under the anger of God. I do not mean that such scrutiny of life is wholly undesirable; depression, though it exaggerates our sinfulness, has a wonderful way of laying its finger on what is amiss, but we must not wilfully continue in sadness; and sadness is often a combination of an old instinct with the staleness which comes of civilised life; and a return to nature, as it is called, is often a cure, because civilisation has this disadvantage, that it often takes from us the necessity of doing many of the things which it is normal to man by inheritance to do—fighting, hunting, preparing food, working with the hands. We combat these old instincts artificially by games and exercises. It is humiliating again to think that golf is an artificial substitute for man's need to hunt and plough, but it is undoubtedly true; and thus to break with the monotony of civilisation, and to delude the mind into believing that it is occupied with primal needs is often a great refreshment. Anyone who fishes and shoots knows that the joy of securing a fish or a partridge is entirely out of proportion to any advantages resulting. A lawyer could make money enough in a single week to buy the whole contents of a fishmonger's shop, but this does not give him half the satisfaction which comes from fishing day after day for a whole week, and securing perhaps three salmon. The fact is that the old savage mind, which lies behind the rational and educated mind, is having its fling; it believes itself to be staving off starvation by its ingenuity and skill, and it unbends like a loosened bow.

We may be enjoying our work, and we may even take glad refuge in it to stave off depression, but we are then often adding fuel to the fire, and tiring the very faculty of resistance, which hardly knows that it needs resting.

The smallest change of scene, of company, of work may effect a miraculous improvement when we are feeling low-spirited and listless. It is not idleness as a rule that we want, but the use of other faculties and powers and muscles.

And thus though our anxieties may be a real factor in our success, and may give us the touch of prudence and vigilance we want, it does not do to allow ourselves to drift into vague fears and dull depressions, and we must fight them in a practical way. We must remember the case of Naaman, who was vexed at being told to go and dip himself in a mud-stained stream running violently in rocky places, when he might have washed in Abana and Pharpar, the statelier, purer, fuller streams of his native land. It is just the little homely torrent that we need, and part of our cares come from being too dignified about them. It is pleasanter to think oneself the battle-ground for high and tragical forces of a spiritual kind, than to realise that some little homely bit of common machinery is out of gear. But we must resist the temptation to feel that our fears have a dark and great significance. We must simply treat them as little sicknesses and ailments of the soul.

I therefore believe that fears are like those little fugitive gliding things that seem to dart across the field of the eye when it is weak and ailing, vague clusters and tangles and spidery webs, that float and fly, and can never be fixed and truly seen; and that they are best treated as we learn to treat common ailments, by not concerning ourselves very much about them, by enduring and evading them and distracting the mind, and not by facing them, because they will not be faced; nor can they be dispelled by reason, because they are not in the plane of reason at all, but phantoms gathered by the sick imagination, distorted out of their proper shape, evil nightmares, the horror of which is gone with the dawn. They are the shadows of our childishness, and they show that we have a long journey before us; and they gain their strength from the fact that we gather them together out of the future like the bundle of sticks in the fable, when we shall have the strength to snap them singly as they come.

The real way to fight them is to get together a treasure of interests and hopes and beautiful visions and emotions, and above all to have some definite work which lies apart from our daily work, to which we can turn gladly in empty hours; because fears are born of inaction and idleness, and melt insensibly away in the warmth of labour and duty.

Nothing can really hurt us except our own despair. But the problem which is difficult is how to practise a real fulness of life, and yet to keep a certain detachment, how to realise that what we do is small and petty enough, but that the greatness lies in our energy and briskness of action; we should try to be interested in life as we are interested in a game, not believing too much in the importance of it, but yet intensely concerned at the moment in playing it as well and skilfully as possible. The happiest people of all are those who can shift their interest rapidly from point to point, and throw themselves into the act of the moment, whatever it may be. Of course this is largely at first a matter of temperament, but temperament is not unalterable; and self-discipline working along the lines of habit has a great attractiveness, the moment we feel that life is beginning to shape itself upon real lines.

XVI

FEAR OF LIFE

LET us divide our fears up into definite divisions, and see how it is best to deal with them. Lowest and worst of all is the shapeless and bodiless fear, which is a real disease of brain and nerves. I know no more poignant description of this than in the strange book *Lavengro*:

"'What ails you, my child,' said a mother to her son, as he lay on a couch under the influence of the dreadful one; 'what ails you? you seem afraid!'

"*Boy*. And so I am; a dreadful fear is upon me.

"*Mother*. But of what? there is no one can harm you; of what are you apprehensive?

"*Boy*. Of nothing that I can express; I know not what I am afraid of, but afraid I am.

"*Mother*. Perhaps you see sights and visions; I knew a lady once who was continually thinking that she saw an armed man threaten her, but it was only an imagination, a phantom of the brain.

"*Boy.* No armed man threatens me; and 'tis not a thing that would cause me any fear. Did an armed man threaten me, I would get up and fight him; weak as I am, I would wish for nothing better, for then, perhaps, I should lose this fear; mine is a dread of I know not what, and there the horror lies.

"*Mother.* Your forehead is cool, and your speech collected. Do you know where you are?

"*Boy.* I know where I am, and I see things just as they are; you are beside me, and upon the table there is a book which was written by a Florentine. All this I see, and that there is no ground for being afraid. I am, moreover, quite cool, and feel no pain—but—but——

"And then there was a burst of 'gemiti, sospiri ed alti guai.' Alas, alas, poor child of clay! as the sparks fly upward, so wast thou born to sorrow—Onward!"

That is a description of amazing power, but of course we are here dealing with a definite brain-malady, in which the emotional centres are directly affected. This in a lesser degree no doubt affects more people than one would wish to think; but it may be considered a physical malady of which fear is the symptom and not the cause.

Let us then frankly recognise the physical element in these irrational terrors; and when one has once done this, a great burden is taken off the mind, because one sees that such fear may be a real illusion, a sort of ghastly mockery, which by directly affecting the delicate machinery through which emotion is translated into act, may produce a symptom of terror which is both causeless and baseless, and which may imply neither a lack of courage nor self-control.

And, therefore, I feel, as against the Ascetic and the Stoic, that I am meant to live and to taste the fulness of life; and that if I begin by choosing the wrong joys, it is that I may learn their unreality. I have learned already to compromise about many things, to be content with getting much less than I desire, to acquiesce in missing many good things altogether. But asceticism for the sake of prudence seems to me a wilful error, as though a man practised starvation through uneasy days, because of the chance that he might some day find himself with not enough to eat. The only self-denial worth practising is the self-denial that one admires, and that seems to one to be fine and beautiful.

For we must emphatically remember that the saint is one who lives life with high enjoyment, and with a vital zest; he chooses holiness because of its irresistible beauty, and because of the appeal it makes to his mind. He does not creep through life ashamed, depressed, anxious, letting ordinary delights slip through his nerveless fingers; and if he denies himself common pleasures, it is because, if indulged, they thwart and mar his purer and more lively joys.

The fear of life, the frame of mind which says, "This attractive and charming thing captivates me, but I will mistrust it and keep it at arm's length, because if I lose it, I shall experience discomfort," seems to me a poor and timid handling of life. I would rather say, "I will use it generously and freely, knowing that it may not endure; but it is a sign to me of God's care for me, that He gives me the desire and the gratification; and even if He means me to learn that it is only a small thing, I can learn that only by using it and trying its sweetness."

This may be held a dangerous doctrine; but I do not mean that life must be a foolish and ingenuous indulgence of every appetite and whim. One must make choices; and there are many appetites which come hand in hand with their own shadow. I am not here speaking of tampering with sin; I think that most people burn their fingers over that in early life. But I am speaking rather of the delights of the body that are in no way sinful, food and drink, games and exercise, love itself; and of the joys of the mind and the artistic sense; free and open relations with men and women of keen interests and eager fancies; the delights of work, professional success, the doing of pleasant tasks as vigorously and as perfectly as one can—all the stir and motion and delight of life.

To shrink back in terror from all this seems to me a sort of cowardice; and it is a cowardice too to go on indulging in things which one does not enjoy for the sake of social tradition. One must not be afraid of breaking with social custom, if one finds that it leads one into dreary and useless formalities, stupid and expensive entertainments, tiresome gatherings, dull and futile assemblies. I think that men and women ought gaily and delightedly to choose the things that minister to their vigour and joy, and to throw themselves willingly into these things, so long as they do not interfere with plainer and simpler duties.

Another way of escape from the importunities of fear is to be very resolute in fighting against our personal claims to honour and esteem. We are sorely wounded through our ambitions, whether they be petty or great; and it is astonishing to find how frail a basis often serves for a sense of dignity. I have known lowly and unimportant people who were yet full of pragmatical self-concern, and whose pride took the form not so much of exalting their own consequence as of thinking meanly of other people. It is easy to restore one's own confidence by dwelling with bitter emphasis on the faults and failings of those about one, by cataloguing the deficiencies of those who have achieved success, by accustoming oneself to think of one's own lack of success as a sign of unworldliness, and by attributing the success of others to a cynical and unscrupulous pursuit of reputation. There is nothing in the world which so differentiates men and women as the tendency to suspect and perceive affronts, and to nurture grièvances. It is so fatally easy to think that one has been inconsiderately treated, and to mistake susceptibility for courage. Let us boldly face the fact that we get in this world very much what we earn and deserve, and there is no surer way of being excluded and left out from whatever is going forward than a habit of claiming more respect and deference than is due to one. If we are snubbed and humiliated, it is generally because we have put ourselves forward and taken more than our share. Whereas if we have been content to bear a hand, to take trouble, and to desire useful work rather than credit, our influence grows silently and we become indispensable. A man who does not notice petty grumbling, who laughs away sharp comments, who does not brood over imagined insults, who forgets irritable passages, who makes allowance for impatience and fatigue, is singularly invulnerable. The power of forgetting is infinitely more valuable than the power of forgiving, in many conjunctions of life. In nine cases out of ten, the wounds which our sensibilities receive are the merest pin-pricks, enlarged and fretted by our own hands; we work the little thorn about in the puncture till it festers, instead of drawing it out and casting it away.

Very few of the prizes of life that we covet are worth winning, if we scheme to get them; it is the honour or the task that comes to us unexpectedly that we deserve. I have heard discontented men say that they never get the particular work that they desire and for which they feel themselves to be suited; and meanwhile life flies swiftly, while we are picturing ourselves in all sorts of coveted situations, and slighting the peaceful happiness, the beautiful joys which lie all around us, as we go forward in our greedy reverie.

I have been much surprised, since I began some years ago to receive letters from all sorts of unknown people, to realise how many persons there are in the world who think themselves unappreciated. Such are not generally people who have tried and failed;—an honest failure very often brings a wholesome sense of incompetence;—but they are generally persons who think that they have never had a chance of showing what is in them, speakers who have found their audiences unresponsive, writers who have been discouraged by finding their amateur efforts unsaleable, men who lament the unsuitability of their profession to their abilities, women who find themselves living in what they call a thoroughly unsympathetic circle. The failure here lies in an incapacity to believe in one's own inefficiency, and a sturdy persuasion of the malevolence of others.

Here is a soil in which fears spring up like thorns and briars. "Whatever I do or say, I shall be passed over and slighted, I shall always find people determined to exclude and neglect me!" I know myself, only too well, how fertile the brain is in discovering almost any reason for a failure except what is generally the real reason, that the work was badly done. And the more eager one is for personal recognition and patent success, the more sickened one is by any hint of contempt and derision.

But it is quite possible, as I also know from personal experience, to go patiently and humbly to work again, to face the reasons for failure, to learn to enjoy work, to banish from the mind the uneasy hope of personal distinction. We may try to discern the humour of Providence, because I am as certain as I can be of anything that we are humorously treated as well as lovingly regarded. Let me relate two small incidents which did me a great deal of good at a time of self-importance. I was once asked to give a lecture, and it was widely announced. I saw my own name in capital letters upon advertisements displayed in the street. On the evening appointed, I went to the place, and met the chairman of the meeting and some of the officials in a room adjoining the hall where I was to speak. We bowed and smiled, paid mutual compliments, congratulated each other on the importance of the occasion. At last the chairman consulted his watch and said it was time to be beginning. A procession was formed, a door was majestically thrown open by an attendant, and we walked with infinite solemnity on to the platform of an entirely empty hall, with rows of benches all wholly unfurnished with guests. I think it was one of the most ludicrous incidents I ever remember. The courteous confusion of the chairman, the dismay of the committee, the colossal nature of the fiasco filled me, I am glad to say, not with mortification, but with an overpowering desire to laugh.

I may add that there had been a mistake about the announcement of the hour, and ten minutes later a minute audience did arrive, whom I proceeded to address with such spirit as I could muster; but I have always been grateful for the humorous nature of the snub administered to me.

Again on another occasion I had to pay a

visit of business to a remote house in the country. A good-natured friend descanted upon the excitement it would be to the household to entertain a living author, and how eagerly my utterances would be listened to. I was received not only without respect but with obvious boredom. In the course of the afternoon I discovered that I was supposed to be a solicitor's clerk, but when a little later it transpired what my real occupations were, I was not displeased to find that no member of the party had ever heard of my existence, or was aware that I had ever published a book, and when I was questioned as to what I had written, no one had ever come across anything that I had printed, until at last I soared into some transient distinction by the discovery that my brother was the author of *Dodo*.

I cannot help feeling that there is something gently humorous about this good-humoured indication that the whole civilised world is not engaged in the pursuit of literature, and that one's claims to consideration depend upon one's social merits. I do honestly think that Providence was here deliberately poking fun at me, and showing me that a habit of presenting one's opinions broadcast to the world does not necessarily mean that the world is much aware either of oneself or of one's opinions.

The cure then, it seems to me, for personal ambition, is the humorous reflection that the stir and hum of one's own particular tee-totum is confined to a very small space and range; and that the witty description of the Greek politician who was said to be well known throughout the whole civilised world and at Lampsacus, or of the philosopher who was announced as the author of many epoch-making volumes and as the second cousin of the Earl of Cork, represents a very real truth, —that reputation is not a thing which is worth bothering one's head about; that if it comes, it is apt to be quite as inconvenient as it is pleasant, while if one grows to depend upon it, it is as liable to part with its sparkle as soda-water in an open glass.

And then if one comes to consider the com-moner claim, the claim to be felt and respected and regarded in one's own little circle, it is wholesome and humiliating to observe how generously and easily that regard is conceded to affectionateness and kindness, and how little it is won by any brilliance or sharpness. Of course irritable, quick-tempered, severe, discontented people can win attention easily enough, and acquire the kind of consideration which is generally conceded to anyone who can be unpleasant. How often families and groups are drilled and cautioned by anxious mothers and sisters not to say or do anything which will vex so-and-so! Such irritable people get the rooms and the chairs and the food that they like, and the talk in their presence is eagerly kept upon subjects on which they can hold forth. But how little such regard lasts, and how welcome a relief it is, when one that is thus courted and deferred to is absent! Of course if one is wholly indifferent whether one is regarded, needed, missed, loved, so long as one can obtain the obedience and the conveniences one likes, there is no more to be said. But I often think of that wonderful poem of Christina Rossetti's about the *revenant*, the spirit that returns to the familiar house, and finds himself unregretted:

> "'To-morrow' and 'to-day,' they cried;
> I was of yesterday!"

One sometimes sees, in the faces of old family servants, in unregarded elderly relatives, bachelor uncles, maiden aunts, who are entertained as a duty, or given a home in charity, a very beautiful and tender look, indescribable in words but unmistakable, when it seems as if self, and personal claims, and pride, and complacency had really passed out of the expression, leaving nothing but a hope of being loved, and a desire to do some humble service.

I saw it the other day in the face of a little old lady, who lived in the house of a well-to-do cousin, with rather a bustling and vigorous family pervading the place. She was a small frail creature, with a tired worn face, but with no look of fretfulness or discontent. She had a little attic as a bedroom, and she was not considered in any way. She effaced herself, ate about as much as a bird would eat, seldom spoke, uttering little ejaculations of surprise and amusement at what was said; if there was a place vacant in the carriage, she drove out. If there was not, she stopped at home. She amused herself by going about in the village, talking to the old women and the children, who half loved and half despised her for being so very unimportant, and for having nothing she could give away. But I do not think the little lady ever had a thought except of gratitude for her blessings, and admiration for the robustness and efficiency of her relations. She claimed nothing from life and expected nothing. It seemed a little frail and vanquished existence, and there was not an atom of what is called proper pride about her; but it was fine, for all that! An infinite sweetness looked out of her eyes; she suffered a good deal, but never complained. She was glad to live, found the world a beautiful and interesting place, and never quarrelled with her slender share of its more potent pleasures. And she will slip silently out of life some day in her attic room; and be strangely mourned and missed. I do not consider that a failure in life, and I am not sure that it is not something much more like a triumph. I know that as I watched her one evening knitting in the corner, following what was said with intense enjoyment, uttering her little bird-like cries, I thought how few of the things that could afflict me had power to wound her, and how little she had to fear. I do not think she wanted to take flight, but yet I am sure she had no dread of death; and when she goes thitherward, leaving the little tired and withered frame behind, it will be just as when the crested lark springs up from the dust of the roadway, and wings his way into the heart of the dewy upland.

XVII

SIMPLICITY

If we are to avoid the dark onset of fear, we must at all costs simplify life, because the more complicated and intricate our life is, and the more we multiply our defences, the more gates and posterns there are by which the enemy can creep upon us. Property, comforts, habits, conveniences, these are the vantage-grounds from which fears can organise their invasions. The more that we need excitement, distraction, diversion, the more helpless we become without them. All this is very clearly recognised and stated in the Gospel. Our Saviour does not seem to regard the abandonment of wealth as a necessary condition of the Christian life, but He does very distinctly say that rich men are beset with great difficulties owing to their wealth, and He indicates that a man who trusts complacently in his possessions is tempted into a disastrous security. He speaks of laying up treasure in heaven as opposed to the treasures which men store up on earth; and He points out that whenever things are put aside unused, in order that the owner may comfort himself by the thought that they are there if he wants them, decay and corruption begin at once to undermine and destroy them. What exactly the treasure in heaven can be it is hard to define. It cannot be anything quite so sordid as good deeds done for the sake of spiritual investment, because our Saviour was very severe on those who, like the Pharisees, sought to acquire righteousness by scrupulosity. Nothing that is done just for the sake of one's own future benefit seems to be regarded in the Gospel as worth doing. The essence of Christian giving seems to be real giving, and not a sort of usurious loan. There is of course one very puzzling parable, that of the unjust steward, who used his last hours in office, before the news of his dismissal could get abroad, in cheating his master, in order to win the favour of the debtors by arbitrarily diminishing the amount of their debts. It seems strange that our Saviour should have drawn a moral out of so immoral an incident. Perhaps he was using a well-known story, and even making allowances for the admiration with which in the East resourcefulness, even of a fraudulent kind, was undoubtedly regarded. But the principle seems clear enough, that if the Christian chooses to possess wealth, he runs a great risk, and that it is therefore wiser to disembarrass oneself of it. Property is regarded in the Gospel as an undoubtedly dangerous thing; but so far from our Lord preaching a kind of socialism, and bidding men to co-operate anxiously for the sake of equalising wealth, He recommends an individualistic freedom from the burden of wealth altogether. But, as always in the Gospel, our Lord looks behind practice to motive; and it is clear that the motive for the abandonment of wealth is not to be a desire to act with a selfish prudence, in order to lay an obligation upon God to repay one generously in the future for present sacrifices, but rather the attainment of an individual liberty, which leaves the spirit free to deal with the real interests of life. And one must not overlook the definite promise that if a man seeks virtue first, even at the cost of earthly possessions and comforts, he will find that they will be added as well.

Those who would discredit the morality of the Gospel would have one believe that our Saviour in dealing with shrewd, homely, literal folk was careful to promise substantial future rewards for any worldly sacrifices they might make; but not so can I read the Gospel. Our Saviour does undoubtedly say plainly that we shall find it worth our while to escape from the burdens and anxieties of wealth, but the reward promised seems rather to be a lightness and contentment of spirit, and a freedom from heavy and unnecessary bonds.

In our complicated civilisation it is far more difficult to say what simplicity of life is. It is certainly not that expensive and dramatic simplicity which is sometimes contrived by people of wealth as a pleasant contrast to elaborate living. I remember the son of a very wealthy man, who had a great mansion in the country and a large house in London, telling me that his family circle were never so entirely happy as when they were living at close quarters in a small Scotch shooting-lodge, where their life was comparatively rough, and luxuries unattainable. But I gathered that the main delight of such a period was the sense of laying up a stock of health and freshness for the more luxurious life which intervened. The Anglo-Saxon naturally loves a kind of feudal dignity; he likes a great house, a crowd of servants and dependants, the impression of power and influence which it all gives; and the delights of ostentation, of having handsome things which one does not use and indeed hardly ever sees, of knowing that others are eating and drinking at one's expense, which is a thing far removed from hospitality, are dear to the temperament of our race. We may say at once that this is fatal to any simplicity of life; it may be that we cannot expect anyone who is born to such splendours deliberately to forego them; but I am sure of this, that a rich man, now and here, who spontaneously parted with his wealth, and lived sparely in a small house, would make perhaps as powerful an appeal to the imagination of the English world as could well be made. If a man had a message to deliver, there could be no better way of emphasizing it. It must not be a mere flight from the anxiety of worldly life into a more congenial seclusion. It should be done as Francis of Assisi did it, by continuing to live the life of the world without any of its normal conveniences. Patent and visible self-sacrifice, if it be accompanied by a tender love of humanity, will always be the most impressive attitude in the world.

But if one is not capable of going to such lengths, if indeed one has nothing that one can resign, how is it possible to practise simplicity of life? It can be done by limiting one's needs, by avoiding luxuries, by having nothing in one's house that one cannot use, by being detached from pretentiousness, by being indifferent to elaborate comforts. There are people whom I know who do this, and who, even though they live with some degree of wealth, are yet themselves obviously independent of comfort to an extraordinary degree. There is a Puritanical dislike of waste which is a very different thing, because it often coexists with an extreme attachment to the particular standard of comfort that the man himself prefers. I know people who believe that a substantial midday meal and a high tea are more righteous than a simple midday meal and a substantial dinner. But the right attitude is one of unconcern and the absence of uneasy scheming as to the details of life. There is no reason why people should not form habits, because method is the primary condition of work; but the moment that habit becomes tyrannous and elaborate, then the spirit is at once in bondage to anxiety. The real victory over these little cares is not for ever to have them on one's mind; or one becomes like the bread-and-butter fly in *Through the Looking-Glass*, whose food was weak tea with cream in it. "But supposing it cannot find any?" said Alice. "Then it dies," says the gnat, who is acting the part of interpreter. "But that must happen very often?" said Alice. "It *always* happens!" says the gnat with sombre emphasis.

Simplicity is, in fact, a difficult thing to lay down rules for, because the essence of it is that it is free from rules; and those who talk and think most about it, are often the most uneasy and complicated natures. But it is certain that if one finds oneself growing more and more fastidious and particular, more and more easily disconcerted and put out and hampered by any variation from the exact scheme of life that one prefers, even if that scheme is an apparently simple one, it is certain that simplicity is at an end. The real simplicity is a sense of being at home and at ease in any company and mode of living, and a quiet equanimity of spirit which cannot be content to waste time over the arrangements of life. Sufficient food and exercise and sleep may be postulated; but these are all to be in the background, and the real occupations of life are to be work and interests and talk and ideas and natural relations with others. One knows of houses where some trifling omission of detail, some failure of service in a meal, will plunge the hostess into a dumb and incommunicable despair. The slightest lapse of the conventional order becomes a cloud that intercepts the sun. But the right attitude to life, if we desire to set ourselves free from this self-created torment, is a resolute avoidance of minute preoccupations, a light-hearted journeying, with an amused tolerance for the incidents of the way. A conventional order of life is useful only in so far as it removes from the mind the necessity of detailed planning, and allows it to flow punctually and mechanically in an ordered course. But if we exalt that order into something sacred and solemn, then we become pharisaical and meticulous, and the savour of life is lost.

One remembers the scene in *David Copperfield* which makes so fine a parable of life; how the merry party who were making the best of an ill-cooked meal, and grilling the chops over the lodging-house fire, were utterly disconcerted and reduced to miserable dignity by the entry of the ceremonious servant with his "Pray, permit me," and how his decorous management of the cheerful affair cast a gloom upon the circle which could not even be dispelled when he had finished his work and left them to themselves.

XVIII

AFFECTION

ONE of the ways in which our fears have power to wound us most grievously is through our affections, and here we are confronted with a real and crucial difficulty. Are we to hold ourselves in, to check the impulses of affection, to use self-restraint, not multiply intimacies, not extend sympathies? One sees every now and then lives which have entwined themselves with every tendril of passion and love and companionship and service round some one personality, and have then been bereaved, with the result that the whole life has been palsied and struck into desolation by the loss. I am thinking now of two instances which I have known; one was a wife, who was childless, and whose whole nature, every motive and every faculty, became centred upon her husband, a man most worthy of love. He died suddenly, and his wife lost everything at one blow; not only her lover and comrade, but every occupation as well which might have helped to distract her, because her whole life had been entirely devoted to her husband; and even the hours when he was absent from her had been given to doing anything and everything that might save him trouble or vexation. She lived on, though she would willingly have died at any moment, and the whole fabric of her life was shattered. Again, I think of a devoted daughter who had done the same office for an old and not very robust father. I heard her once say that the sorrow of her mother's death had been almost nullified for her by finding that she could do everything for and be everything to her father, whom she almost adored. She had refused an offer of marriage from a man whom she sincerely loved, that she might not leave her father, and she never even told her father of the incident, for fear that he might have felt that he had stood in the way of her happiness. When he died, she too found herself utterly desolate, without ties and without occupation, an elderly woman almost without friends or companions.

Ought one to feel that this kind of jealous absorption in a single individual affection is a mistake? It certainly brought both the wife and daughter an intense happiness, but in both cases the relation was so close and so intimate that it tended gradually to seclude them from all other relations. The husband and the father were both reserved and shy men, and desired no other companionship. One can see so easily how it all came about, and what the inevitable result was bound to be, and yet it would have been difficult at any point to say what could have been done. Of course these great absorbed emotions involve large risks; and it may be doubted whether life can be safely lived on these intensive lines. These are of course extreme instances, but there are many cases in the world, and especially in the case of women whose life is entirely built up on certain emotions like the love and care of children; and when that is so, a nature becomes liable to the sharpest incursions of fear. It is of little use arguing such cases theoretically, because, as the proverb says, as the land lies the water flows,—and love makes very light of all prudential considerations.

The difficulty does not arise with large and generous natures which give love prodigally in many directions, because if one such relation is broken by death, love can still exercise itself upon those that remain. It is the fierce and jealous sort of love that is so hard to deal with, a love that exults in solitariness of devotion, and cannot bear any intrusion of other relations.

Yet if one believes, as I for one believe, that the secret of the world is somehow hidden in love, and can be interpreted through love alone, then one must run the risks of love, and seek for strength to bear the inevitable suffering which love must bring.

But men and women are very differently made in this respect. Among innumerable minor differences, certain broad divisions are clear. Men, in the first place, both by training and temperament, are far less dependent upon affection than women. Career and occupation play a much larger part in their thoughts. If one could test and intercept the secret and unoccupied reveries of men, when the mind moves idly among the objects which most concern it, it would be found, I do not doubt, that men's minds occupy themselves much more about definite and tangible things—their work, their duties, their ambitions, their amusements—and centre little upon the thought of other people; an affection, an emotional relation, is much more of an incident than a settled preoccupation; and then with men there are two marked types, those who give and lavish affection freely, who are interested and attracted by others and wish to attach and secure close friends; and there are others who respond to advances, yet do not go in search of friendship, but only accept it when it comes; and the singular thing is that such natures, which are often cold and self-absorbed, have a power of kindling emotion in others which men of generous and eager feeling sometimes lack. It is strange that it should be so, but there is some psychological law at the back of it; and it is certainly true in my experience that the men who have been most eagerly sought in friendship have not as a rule been the most open-hearted and expansive natures. I suppose that a certain law of pursuit holds good, and that people of self-contained temperament, with a sort of baffling charm, who are critical and hard to please, excite a certain ambition in those who would claim their affection.

Women, I have no doubt, live far more in the thought of others, and desire their intention; they wish to arrive at mutual understanding and confidence, to explore personality, to pierce behind the surface, to establish a definite relation. Yet in the matter of relations with others, women are often, I believe, less sentimental, and even less tender-hearted than men, and they have a far swifter and truer intuition of character. Though the two sexes can never really understand each other's point of view, because no imagination can cross the gulf of fundamental difference, yet I am certain that women understand men far better than men understand women. The whole range of motives is strangely different, and men can never grasp the comparative unimportance with which women regard the question of occupation. Occupation is for men a definite and isolated part of life, a thing important and absorbing in itself, quite apart from any motives or reasons. To do something, to make something, to produce something—that desire is always there, whatever ebb and flow of emotions there may be; it is an end in itself with men, and with many women it is not so; for women mostly regard work as a necessity, but not an interesting necessity. In a woman's occupation, there is generally someone at the end of it, for whom and in connection with whom it is done. This is probably largely the result of training and tradition, and great changes are now going on in the direction of women finding occupations for themselves. But take the case of such a profession as teaching; it is quite possible for a man to be an effective and competent teacher, without feeling any particular interest in the temperaments of his pupils, except in so far as they react upon the work to be done. But a woman can hardly take this impersonal attitude; and this makes women both more and less effective, because human beings invariably prefer to be dealt with dispassionately; and this is as a rule more difficult for women; and thus in a complicated matter affecting conduct, a woman as a rule forms a sounder judgment on what has actually occurred than a man, and is perhaps more likely to take a severe view. The attitude of a Galileo is often a useful one for a teacher, because boys and girls ought in matters that concern themselves to learn how to govern themselves.

Thus in situations involving relation with others, women are more liable to feel anxiety and the pressure of personal responsibility; and the question is to what extent this ought to be indulged, in what degree men and women ought to assume the direction of other lives, and whether it is wholesome for the director to allow a desire for personal dominance to be substituted for more spontaneous motives.

It very often happens that the temperaments which most claim help and support are actuated by the egotistical desire to find themselves interesting to others, while those who willingly assume the direction of other lives are attracted more by the sense of power than by genuine sympathy.

But it is clear that it is in the region of our affections that the greatest risks of all have to be run. By loving, we render ourselves liable to the darkest and heaviest fears. Yet here, I believe, we ought to have no doubt at all; and the man who says to himself, "I should like to bestow my affection on this person and on that, but I will keep it in restraint, because I am afraid of the suffering which it may entail,"—such a man, I say, is very far from the kingdom of God. Because love is the one quality which, if it reaches a certain height, can altogether despise and triumph over fear. When ambition and delight and energy fail, love can accompany us, with hope and confidence, to the dark gate; and thus it is the one thing about which we can hardly be mistaken. If love does not survive death, then life is built upon nothingness, and we may be glad to get away; but it is more likely that it is the only thing that does survive.

XIX

SIN

It is every one's duty to take himself seriously—that is the right mean between taking oneself either solemnly or apologetically. There is no merit in being apologetic about oneself. One has a right to be there, wherever one is, a right to an opinion, a right to take some kind of a hand in whatever is going on; natural tact is the only thing which can tell us exactly how far those rights extend; but it is inconvenient to be apologetic, because if one insists on explaining how one comes to be there, or how one comes to have an opinion, other people begin to think that one needs explanation and excuse; but it is even worse to be solemn about oneself, because English people are very critical in private, though they are tolerant in public, because they dislike a scene, and have not got the art of administering the delicate snub which indicates to a man that his self-confidence is exuberant without humiliating him ; when English people inflict a snub, they do it violently and emphatically, like Dr. Johnson, and it generally means that they are relieving themselves of accumulated disapproval. An Englishman is apt to be deferential, and one of the worst temptations of official life is the temptation to be solemn. There is an old story about Scott and Wordsworth, when the latter stayed at Abbotsford ; Scott, during the whole visit, was full of little pleasant and courteous allusions to Wordsworth's poems ; and one of the guests present records how at the end of the visit not a single word had ever passed Wordsworth's lips which could have indicated that he knew his host to have ever written a line of poetry or prose.

I was sitting the other day at a function next a man of some eminence, and I was really amazed at the way in which he discoursed of himself and his habits, his diet, his hours of work, and the blank indifference with which he received similar confidences. He merely waited till the speaker had finished, and then resumed his own story.

It is this sort of solemn egotism which makes us overvalue our anxieties quite out of all proportion to their importance, because they all appear to us as integral elements of a dignified drama in which we enact the hero's part. We press far too heavily on the sense of responsibility ; and if we begin by telling boys, as is too often done in sermons, that whatever they do or say is of far-reaching consequence, that every lightest word may produce an effect, that any carelessness of speech or example may have disastrous effects upon the character of another, we are doing our best to encourage the self-emphasis which is the very essence of priggishness.

There is a curious conflict going on at the present time in English life between light-mindedness and solemnity; there is a great appetite for living, a love of amusement, a tendency to subordinate the interests of the future to the pleasure of the moment, and to think that the one serious evil is boredom; that is a healthy manifestation enough in its way, because it stands for interest and delight in life; but there is another strain in our nature, that of a rather heavy pietism, inherited from our Puritan ancestors. It must not be forgotten that the Puritan got a good deal of interest out of his sense of sin; as the old combative elements of feudal ages disappeared, the soldierly blood retained the fighting instinct, and turned it into moral regions. The sense of adventure is impelled to satiate itself, and the *Pilgrim's Progress* is a clear enough proof that the old combativeness was all there, revelling in danger, and exulting in the thought that the human being was in the midst of foes. Sin represented itself to the Puritan as a thing out of which he could get a good deal of fun; not the fun of yielding to it, but the fun of whipping out his sword and getting in some shrewd blows. When preachers nowadays lament that we have lost the sense of sin, what they really mean is that we have lost our combativeness: we no longer believe that we must treat our foes with open and brutal violence, and we perceive that such conduct is only pitting one sin against another. There is no warrant in the Gospel for the combative idea of the Christian life; all such metaphors and suggestions come from St. Paul and the Apocalypse. The fact is that the world was not ready for the utter peaceableness of the Gospel, and it had to be accommodated to the violence of the world.

Now again the Christian idea is coloured by scientific and medical knowledge, and sin, instead of an enemy which we must fight, has become a disease which we must try to cure.

Sins, the ordinary sins of ordinary life, are not as a rule instincts which are evil in themselves, so much as instincts which are selfishly pursued to the detriment of others; sin is in its essence the selfishness which will not co-operate, and which secures advantages unjustly, without any heed to the disadvantage of others. *Sympathetic imagination* is the real foe of sin, the power of putting oneself in the place of another; and much of the sentiment which is so prevalent nowadays is the evidence of the growth of sympathy.

The old theory of sin lands one in a horrible dilemma, because it implies a treacherous enmity on the part of God, to create man weak and unstable, and to pit his weakness against tyrannous desires; to allow his will to do evil to be stronger than his power to do right, is a satanical device. One must not sacrifice the truth to the desire for simplicity and effective statement. The truth is intricate and obscure, and to pretend that it is plain and obvious is mere hypocrisy. The strength of Calvinism is its horrible resemblance to a natural inference from the facts of life; but if any sort of Calvinism is true, then it is a mere insult to the intelligence to say that God is loving or just. The real basis for all deep-seated fear about life is the fear that one will not be dealt with either lovingly or justly. But we have to make a simple choice as to what we will believe, and the only hope is to believe that immediate harshness and injustice is not ultimately inconsistent with Love. No one who knows anything of the world and of life can pretend to think or say that suffering always results from, or is at all proportioned to, moral faults; and if we are tempted to regard all our disasters as penal consequences, then we are tempted to endure them with gloomy and morbid immobility.

It is far more wholesome and encouraging to look upon many disasters that befall us as opportunities to show a little spirit, to evoke the courage which does not come by indolent prosperity, to increase our sympathy, to enlarge our experience, to make things clearer to us, to develop our mind and heart, to free us from material temptations. Past suffering is not always an evil, it is often an exciting reminiscence. It is good to take life adventurously, like Odysseus of old. What would one feel about Odysseus if, instead of contriving a way out of the Cyclops' cave, he had set himself to consider of what forgotten sin his danger was the consequence? Suffering and disaster come to us to develop our inventiveness and our courage, not to daunt and dismay us; and we ought therefore to approach experience with a sense of humour, if possible, and with a lively curiosity. I recollect hearing a man the other day describing an operation to which he had been subjected. "My word," he said, his eyes sparkling with delight at the recollection, "that was awful, when I came into the operating-room, and saw the surgeons in their togs, and the pails and basins all about, and was invited to step up to the table!" There is nothing so agreeable as the remembrance of fears through which we have passed; and we can only learn to despise them by finding out how unbalanced they were.

I do not mean that fears can ever be pleasant at the time, but we do them too much honour if we court them and defer to them. However much we may be tortured by them, there is always something at the back of our mind which despises our own susceptibility to them; and it is that deeper instinct which we ought to trust.

But we cannot even begin to trust it, as long as we allow ourselves to believe pietistically that the Mind of God is set on punishment. That is the ghastly error which humanity tends to make. It has been dinned into us, alas, from our early years, and religious phraseology is constantly polluted by it Our Saviour lent no countenance to this at all; He spoke perfectly plainly against the theory of "judgments." Of course suffering is sometimes a consequence of sin, but it is not a vindictive punishment; it is that we may learn our mistake. But we must give up the revengeful idea of God: that is imported into our scale of values by the grossest anthropomorphism. Only the weak man, who fears that his safety will be menaced if he does not make an example, deals in revenge. He is indignant at anything which mortifies his vanity, which implies any doubt of his power or any disregard of his wishes. Revenge is born of terror, and to think of God as vindictive is to think of Him as subject to fear. Serene and unquestioned strength can have nothing to do with fear. Milton is largely responsible for perpetuating this belief. He makes the Almighty say to the Son—

> "Let us advise, and to this hazard draw
> With speed what force is left, and all employ
> In our defence, lest unawares we lose
> This our high place, our sanctuary, our hill."

Milton's idea of the Almighty was frankly that of a Power who had undertaken more than he could manage, and who had allowed things to go too far. But it is a puerile conception of God; and to allow ourselves to think or speak of God as a Power that has to take precautions, or that has anything to fear from the exercise of human volition, is to cloud the whole horizon at once.

But we ought rather to think of God as a Power which for some reason works through imperfection. The battle of the world is that of force against inertness: and our fears are the shadow of that combat.

Fear should then rather show us that we are being confronted with experience; and that our duty is to disregard it, to march forward through it, to come out on the other side of it. It is all an adventure, in fact! The disaster in which we are involved is not sent to show us that the Eternal Power which created us is vexed at our failures, or bent on crushing us. It is exactly the opposite; it is to show us that we are worth testing, worth developing, and that we are to have the glory of going on; the very fear of death is the last test of our belief in Love. We are assuredly meant to believe that the coward is to learn the beauty of courage, that the laggard is to perceive the worth of energy, that the selfish man is to be taught sympathy. If we must take a metaphor, let us rather think of God as the graver of the gem than as the child that beats her doll for collapsing instead of sitting upright.

It is our dishonouring thought of God as jealous, suspicious, fond of exhibiting power, revengeful, cruel, that does us harm. We must rather think of His Heart as full of courage, energy, and hope; as teeming with joy, lightness, zest, mirth; and then we can begin to think of failures, fears, delays as things small and unimportant, not as malicious ambushes, but as rough bits of road, as obstacles to reveal and to develop our strength and gaiety. There is no joy in the world so great as the joy of finding ourselves stronger than we know; and that is what God is bent upon showing us, and not upon proving to us that we are vile and base, in the spirit of the old Calvinist who said to his own daughter when she was dying of a painful disease, that she must remember that all short of Hell was mercy. It is so; but Hell is rather what we start from, and out of which we have to find our way, than the waste-paper basket of life, the last receptacle for our shattered purposes.

XX

SERENITY

To achieve serenity we must have the power of keeping our hearts and minds fixed upon something which is beyond and above the passing incidents of life, which so disconcert and overshadow us, and which are after all but as clouds in the sky, or islets in a great ocean. Think with what smiling indifference a man would meet indignation and abuse and menace, if he were aware that an hour hence he would be triumphantly vindicated and applauded. How calmly would a man sleep in a condemned cell if he knew that a free pardon were on its way to him! Of course the more eagerly and enjoyably we live, so much the more we are affected by little incidents, beyond which we can hardly look when they bring us so much pleasure or so much discomfort; and thus it is always the men and women of keen and highly-strung natures, who taste the quality of every moment, in its sweetness and its bitterness, who will most feel the influence of fear. Edward FitzGerald once sadly confessed that, as life went on, days of perfect delight—a beautiful scene, a melodious music, the society of those whom he loved best—brought him less and less joy, because he felt that they were passing swiftly, and could not be recalled. And of course the imaginative nature which lives tremulously in delight will be most apt to portend sadness in hours of happiness, and in sorrow to anticipate the continuance of sorrow. That is an inevitable effect of temperament; but we must not give way helplessly to temperament, or allow ourselves to drift wherever the mind bears us. Just as the skilled sailor can tack up against the wind, and use ingenuity to compel a contrary breeze to bring him to the haven of his desire, so we must be wise in trimming our sails to the force of circumstance; while there is an eager delight in making adverse conditions help us to realise our hopes.

The timid soul that loves delight is apt to say

to itself, " I am happy now in health and circumstances and friends, but I lean out into the future, and see that health must fail and friends must drift away; death must part me from those I love; and beyond all this, I see the cloudy gate through which I must myself pass, and I do not know what lies beyond it." That is true enough! It is like the story of the old prince, as told by Herodotus, who said in his sorrowful age that the Gods gave man only a taste of life, just enough to let him feel that life was sweet, and then took the cup from his lips. But if we look fairly at life, at our own life, at other lives, we see that pleasure and contentment, even if we hardly realised that it was contentment at the time, have largely predominated over pain and unhappiness; a man must be very rueful and melancholy before he will deliberately say that life has not been worth living, though I suppose that there have probably been hours in the lives of all of us when we have thought and said and even believed that we would rather not have lived at all than suffer so. Neither must we pass over the fact that every day there are men and women who, under the pressure of calamity and dismay, bring their lives to a voluntary end.

But we have to be very dull and thankless and slow of heart not to feel that by being allowed to live, for however short a time, we have been allowed to take part in a very beautiful and wonderful thing. The loveliness of earth, its colours, its lights, its scents, its savours, the pleasures of activity and health, the sharp joys of love and friendship, these are surely very great and marvellous experiences, and the Mind which planned them must be full of high purpose, eager intention, infinite goodwill. And we may go further than that, and see that even our sorrows and failures have often brought something great to our view, something which we feel we have learned and apprehended, something which we would not have missed, and which we cannot do without. If we will frankly recognise all this, we cannot feebly crumple up at the smallest touch of misery, and say suspiciously and vindictively that we wish we had never opened our eyes upon the world; and even if we do say that, even if we abandon ourselves to despair, we yet cannot hope to escape; we did not enter life by our own will, it is not our own prudence that has kept us there, and even if we end it voluntarily, as Carlyle said, by noose or henbane, we cannot for an instant be sure that we are ending it; every inference in the world, in fact, would tend to indicate that we do not end it. We cannot destroy matter, we can only disperse and rearrange it; we cannot generate a single force, we can only summon it from elsewhere, and concentrate it, as we concentrate electricity, at a single glowing point. Force seems as indestructible as matter, and there is no reason to think that life is destructible either. So that if we are to resign ourselves to any belief at all, it must be to the belief that "to be, or not to be" is not a thing which is in our power at all. We may extinguish life, as we put out a light; but we do not destroy it, we only rearrange it.

And we can thus at least practise and exercise ourselves in the belief that we cannot bring our experiences to an end, however petulantly and irritably we desire to do so, because it simply is not in our power to effect it. We talk about the power of the will, but no effort of will can obliterate the life that we have lived, or add a cubit to our stature; we cannot abrogate any law of nature, or destroy a single atom of matter. What it seems that we can do with the will is to make a certain choice, to select a certain line, to combine existing forces, to use them within very small limits. We can oblige ourselves to take a certain course, when every other inclination is reluctant to do it; and even so the power varies in different people. It is useless then to depend blindly upon the will, because we may suddenly come to the end of it, as we may come to the end of our physical forces. But what the will can do is to try certain experiments, and the one province where its function seems to be clear, is where it can discover that we have often a reserve of unsuspected strength, and more courage and power than we had supposed. We can certainly oppose it to bodily inclinations, whether they be seductions of sense or temptations of weariness. And in this one respect the will can give us, if not serenity, at least a greater serenity than we expect.

We can use the will to endure, to wait, to suspend a hasty judgment; and impulse is the thing which menaces our serenity most of all. The will indeed seems to be like a little weight which we can throw into either scale. If we have no doubt how we ought to act, we can use the will to enforce our judgment, whether it is a question of acting or of abstaining; if we are in doubt how to act, we can use our will to enforce a wise delay.

The truth then about the will is that it is a force which we cannot measure, and that it is as unreasonable to say that it does not exist as to say that it is unlimited. It is foolish to describe it as free; it is no more free than a prisoner in a cell is free; but yet he has a certain power to move about within his cell, and to choose among possible employments.

Anyone who will deliberately test his will, will find that it is stronger than he suspects; what often weakens our use of it is that we are so apt to look beyond the immediate difficulty into a long perspective of imagined obstacles, and to say within ourselves, "Yes, I may perhaps achieve this immediate step, but I cannot take step after step—my courage will fail!" Yet if one does make the immediate effort, it is common to find the whole range of obstacles modified by the single act; and thus the first step towards the attainment of serenity of life is to practise cutting off the vista of possible contingencies from our view, and to create a habit of dealing with a case as it occurs.

I am often tempted myself to send my anxious mind far ahead in vague dismay; at the beginning of a week crammed with various engagements, numerous tasks, constant labour, little businesses, many of them with their own attendant anxiety, it is easy to say that there is no time to do anything that one wants to do, and to feel that the matters themselves will be handled amiss and bungled. But if one can only keep the mind off, or distract it by work, or beguile it by a book, a walk, a talk, how easily the thread spins off the reel, how quietly one comes to harbour on the Saturday evening, with everything done and finished!

Again, I am personally much disposed to

dread the opposition and the displeasure of colleagues, and to shrink nervously from anything which involves dealing with a number of people. I ought to have found out before now how futile such dread is; other people forget their vexation and even grow ashamed of it, much as one does oneself; and looking back I can recall no crisis which turned out either as intricate or as difficult as one expected.

Let me admit that I have more than once in life made grave mistakes through this timidity and indolence, or through an imaginativeness which could see in a great opportunity nothing but a sea of troubles, which would, I do not doubt, have melted away as one advanced. But no one has suffered except myself! Institutions do not depend upon individuals; and I regard such failures now just as the petulant casting away of a chance of experience, as a lesson which I would not learn; but there is nothing irreparable about it; one only comes, more slowly and painfully, to the same goal at last. I dare not say that I regret it all, for we are all of us, whether small or great, being taught a mighty truth, whether we wish it or know it; and all that we can do to hasten it is to put our will into the right scale. I do not think mistakes and failures ought to trouble one much; at all events there is no fear mingled with them. But I do not here claim to have attained any real serenity—my own heart is too impatient, too fond of pleasure for that!—yet I can see clearly enough that it is there, if I could but grasp it; and I know well enough how it is to be attained, by being content to wait, and by realising at every instant and moment of life that, in spite of my tremors and indolences, my sharp impatiences, my petulant disgusts, something very real and great is being shown me, which I shall at last, however dimly, perceive; and that even so the goal of the journey is far beyond any horizon that I can conceive, and built up like the celestial city out of unutterable brightness and clearness, upon a foundation of peace and joy.

It is very difficult to determine, by any exercise of the intellect or imagination, what fears would remain to us if we were freed from the dominion of the body. All material fears and anxieties would come to an end; we should no longer have any poverty to dread, or any of the limitations or circumscriptions which the lack of the means of life inflicts upon us; we should have no ambitions left, because the ambitions which centre on influence—that is, upon the desire to direct and control the interests of a nation or a group of individuals—have no meaning apart from the material framework of civil life. The only kind of influence which would survive would be the influence of emotion, the direct appeal which one who lives a higher and more beautiful life can make to all unsatisfied souls, who would fain find the way to a greater serenity of mood. Even upon earth we can see a faint foreshadowing of this in the fact that the only personalities who continue to hold the devotion and admiration of humanity are the idealists. Men and women do not make pilgrimages to the graves and houses of eminent jurists and bankers, political economists or statisticians: these have done their work, and have had their reward. Even the monuments of statesmen and conquerors have little power to touch the imagination, unless some love for humanity, some desire to uplift and benefit the race, have entered into their schemes and policies. No, it is rather the soil which covers the bones of dreamers and visionaries that is sacred yet, prophets and poets, artists and musicians, those who have seen through life to beauty, and have lived and suffered that they might inspire and tranquillise human hearts. The princes of the earth, popes and emperors, lie in pompous sepulchres, and the thoughts of those who regard them, as they stand in metal or marble, dwell most on the vanity of earthly glory. But at the tombs of men like Vergil and Dante, of Shakespeare and Michelangelo, the human heart still trembles into tears, and hates the death that parts soul from soul. So that if, like Dante, we could enter the shadow-land, and hold converse with the spirits of the dead, we should seek out to consort with, not those who have subdued and wasted the earth, or have terrified men into obedience and service, but those whose hearts were touched by dreams of impossible beauty, and who have taught us to be kind and compassionate and tender-hearted, to love God and our neighbour, and to detect, however faintly, the hope of peace and joy which binds us all together.

And thus if emotion, by which I mean the power of loving, is the one thing which survives, the fears which may remain will be concerned with all the thoughts which cloud love, the anger and suspicion that divide us; so that perhaps the only fears which will survive at all will be the fears of our own selfishness and coldness, that inner hardness which has kept us from the love of God and isolated us from our neighbour. The pride which kept us from admitting that we were wrong, the jealousy that made us hate those who won the love we could not win, the baseness which made us indifferent to the discomfort of others if we could but secure our own ease, these are the thoughts which may still have the power to torture us; and the hell that we may have to fear may be the hell of conscious weakness and the horror of retrospect, when we recollect how under these dark skies of earth we went on our way claiming and taking all that we could get, and disregarding love for fear of being taken advantage of. One of the grievous fears of life is the fear of seeing ourselves as we really are, in all our baseness and pettiness; yet that will assuredly be shown us in no vindictive spirit, but that we may learn to rise and soar.

There is no hope that death will work an immediate moral change in us; it may set us free from some sensual and material temptations, but the innermost motives will indeed survive, that instinct which makes us again and again pursue what we know to be false and unsatisfying.

The more that we shrink from self-knowledge, the more excuses that we make for ourselves, the more that we tend to attribute our failures to our circumstances and to the action of others, the more reason we have to fear the revelation of death. And the only way to face that is to keep our minds open to any light, to nurture and encourage the wish to be different, to pray hour by hour that at any cost we may be taught the truth; it is useless to search for happy illusions, to look for short cuts, to hope vaguely that strength and virtue will burst out like a fountain beside our path. We have a long and toilsome way to travel, and we can by no device abbreviate it; but when we suffer and grieve, we are walking more swiftly to our goal; and the hours we spend in fear, in sending the mind in weariness along the desolate track, are merely wasted, for we can alter nothing so. We use life best when we live it eagerly, exulting in its fulness and its significance, casting ourselves into strong relations with others, drinking in beauty, making high music in our hearts. There is an abundance of awe in the experiences through which we pass, awe at the greatness of the vision, at the vastness of the design, as it embraces and enfolds our weakness. But we are inside it all, an integral and indestructible part of it; and the shadow of fear falls when we doubt this, when we dread being overlooked or disregarded. No such thing can happen to us; our inheritance is absolute and certain, and it is fear that keeps us away from it, and the fear of fearlessness. For we are contending not with God, but with the fear which hides Him from our shrinking eyes; and our prayer should be the undaunted prayer of Moses in the clefts of the mountain, "I beseech Thee, show me Thy Glory!"

THE END